Mark A. McNeil

All in the Name

How the Bible Led Me to Faith
in the Trinity and the Catholic Church

Published by Catholic Answers, Inc.
2020 Gillespie Way
El Cajon, California 92020
1-888-291-8000 orders
619-387-0042 fax
catholic.com

Printed in the United States of America

Cover design by ebooklaunch.com
Interior design by Russell Graphic Design

978-1-68357-100-1
978-1-68357-101-8 Kindle
978-1-68357-102-5 ePub

Contents

Acknowledgements

The sounds of a quiet beach have a healing effect on me. I sometimes think of our lives as a journey to a faraway beach we have only heard of but never actually seen. Imagine that you had never directly experienced the waves, the birds, the sand, the warm waters, or the occasional jumping fish. As you drive toward this beach, there are many temptations to settle for something less. Perhaps a swimming pool at a hotel or some other attraction. But you persist in your journey. When you finally arrive at the beach, you don't stick your toe in the waters, look around and then declare, "Time to go home—we've now seen the beach!" The journey has only just begun. There are new experiences to be had as you explore the waters, soak in the sun, play with your family members, and take walks as the sun sets or rises.

We are always in motion. The difference between now and what we call "heaven" is that we now live in faith and hope, moving toward a happiness that we cannot find in any created thing. Heaven is our final arrival at the reality that we were always desiring, whether we realize it or not. Once we arrive, however, we are not finished. Knowing and loving God is never static or boring. To say one is bored with God is to admit that he does not know what "God" means. In my parable, God is the boundless ocean in which we will endlessly wade throughout eternity without ever exhausting its riches and joys.

A good part of this book will focus on the mystery of the Trinity. As hard as it may be to grasp, God is love. God is radical, self-giving love. To be God is to exist in supreme happiness on account of this perfect love. The Father is self-emptying love, and that is the reason why there is a Son. The Father and Son together are self-emptying love, and that is why there is a Holy Spirit. The core of heavenly life is to see and understand that the only thing that *must* always be is infinite love. Since we are made in the "image" of this God, until we learn that the key to happiness is love, we are unhappy and confused. The constant tension between "settling for something less" and entering into the eternal mystery of trinitarian love is a big part of what creates the drama of each of our lives.

It is also true that we cannot know our own selves without reference to those persons who journey along with us in this life. It is a deeply trinitarian truth that we cannot understand or even have a real sense of ourselves without the other persons in our lives. The potentialities within us are actualized as we are challenged, taught, disappointed, encouraged, rebuked, consoled, loved, and even, on occasion, rejected.

The list of those persons who have enabled me to have a sense of my own identity is a long one. This includes not only those who supported my journey to the Catholic Church but also those who deeply disagree with me. The influence of family, friends, colleagues, priests, teachers, fellow parishioners, and students has been and continues to be inestimable.

The community of Strake Jesuit College Preparatory in Houston is not merely my place of employment but also truly my vocational home. The many people that make that community so great have a very special place in my heart. Our parish community of St. Luke the Evangelist includes some of the finest Christians around and brings great joy to our family.

To all my companions in life who may read these words, thank you.

I offer a special thanks to those many friends I only know through their written words. Books have long had a special place in my life, and the many minds I have encountered through their writings have had an immeasurable impact.

For their willingness to leave their ideas behind in the form of words, even when I disagree with them, I am grateful.

Finally, I wish to express the highest gratitude to my family. Our daily journey together is my greatest joy. The greatest treasure I have to give you is Jesus Christ. My life will have been a success if you always embrace this treasure with me.

To my wife, Patti: Thank you for sharing your amazing heart of love with me. I'm so grateful we are able to help each other to heaven each day. Words are too weak to express how much your husband, children, and countless others love you.

Introduction

A Conversation and a Conversion†

In 1983, at thirteen years of age, I walked into a United Pentecostal church and had the experience of "speaking in tongues."‡ I was then taken, along with my mom and sister, to a baptismal tank and baptized "in the name of Jesus." All of this took place at a "revival" service we attended at the invitation of a lady my mother knew from work.

My family attended a Southern Baptist church in those days. Although we were not associated with a church in my earliest years, I heard the story of God's love for us, demonstrated in Jesus Christ, and fell in love with it. This led to a passion to read the Bible and, encouraged by the Baptists in my life, to look for opportunities to share the good news with others. I was heavily involved in our youth group, and my pastor very much encouraged the "call to preach" that I had recently professed. The "call to preach" is a Baptist way of talking about a vocation to ministry.

Another similarly minded youth at the church, Ronnie, shared my enthusiasm. We could be seen at school carrying

---

† The word *conversion* is used here in the sense of any major shift of religious convictions. Conversion, in this usage, is not necessarily a positive development.

‡ Throughout this work the word *church* refers to any body of professing Christians. I will capitalize this word when referring to the Catholic Church or to the historical Tradition expressed most fully in the Catholic Church. From a Catholic perspective, the word *church* is reserved for those communions that have legitimate apostolic succession and the fullness of the sacrament of the Eucharist. Catholicism does not deny that meaningful elements of Christianity exist outside Catholicism, but the word *Church* is a technical one that cannot be extended indefinitely without compromising the full meaning of the Church as established by Christ. I use this term, then, in a loose sense in accord with the manner of speaking commonly found in the movements I am evaluating. If I were concerned with technical language, "ecclesial communion" would better express the intended meaning.

11

our bibles and, when the opportunity presented itself, sharing our understanding of the Christian faith. My experience of speaking in tongues and my rebaptism "in the name of Jesus" were tucked away in my memory, but they did not immediately affect my church attendance or growing desire to spend my life in ministry among the Baptists. I was simply not sure what to make of this experience.

Some months later, shortly after I began high school, another freshman youth, Ricky, noticed I had a Bible. Ricky was an enthusiastic, albeit somewhat mischievous, young man. After initiating a conversation on religious matters, he invited me to a church he had recently begun attending with his family. It turned out this was the very church at which I had the experiences mentioned earlier (speaking in tongues and baptism "in Jesus' name"). He invited me to a youth service at the church the upcoming Friday evening. I talked my mom into allowing me to attend.

When I walked into the building, I found no youths. I questioned a middle-aged, balding man whose office door was slightly ajar. He explained that the youth were meeting at someone's house that evening and then questioned me about my background.

"I go to a Baptist church but was invited by a friend of mine at school to come to a youth group meeting here tonight," I explained. He then questioned me about my Baptist faith. I did my best. I had memorized a small arsenal of texts supporting basic theological claims we made.

The subject quickly turned to baptism. He gently asked, "Did you know that the early Christians baptized in the name of Jesus *only*?" I was able to locate Matthew 28:19 and explain that this text indicates baptism is performed "in the name of the Father, Son, and Holy Spirit."† He patiently explained, with a grin, "The 'name' of the Father, Son, and Holy Spirit is Jesus! 'Father' is not a name. We call many people fathers. This is a *title*, not a name," he reasoned. "According to John 5:43, the Father's name is Jesus!" Who would argue against the conclusion that the Son's name is Jesus? He cited Matthew 1:21 in support.

"The Holy Spirit, too, has the name Jesus (John 14:26). Since Jesus came 'in his Father's name' and the Holy Spirit is sent in the name of Jesus, it follows that baptism in the *name*, singular, of the Father, Son, and Holy Spirit is none other than baptism in the name of *Jesus*." The clinching observation on this subject was a barrage of texts from the book of Acts that appear to confirm this conclusion (Acts 2:38, 8:16, 10:48, 19:5). "Where," he asked, "is there any indication that people were baptized *saying*, 'in the name of the Father, Son, and Holy Spirit'?"

His reasoning seemed quite cogent. He then took me a step further. "Where is the word *Trinity* in the Bible?" I recalled reading somewhere that the *word* was not in the Bible but that the *concept* was. I mustered a text or two in support. He quickly dismissed my understanding of those texts, showing me reasonable alternative interpretations. He patiently explained that the Bible emphatically teaches there is only one God (Deut. 6:4). The Bible affirms and insists that Jesus is God, he reasoned, but he was also a man. It is this *dual nature* of Jesus that explains the many biblical texts that trinitarians offer that *seem* to suggest there is more than one who is God.

---

† Biblical citations, unless otherwise indicated, are taken from the *New American Standard* translation of the Bible (The Lockman Foundation, 1977). This choice was based on (a) the fact that this translation emphasizes literal communication of meaning in contrast to dynamic equivalence, certainly a desired feature in a work like this, (b) it is not a specifically Catholic translation, and (c) it is highly regarded among many Protestants and Evangelicals, including Pentecostals, who might read this work.

References to the *Father* refer to the *divinity* of Jesus while references to the *Son* refer to his *humanity*. When Jesus prays to the Father, for instance, we should understand this as communication between the human nature and the divine.[†] It would be absurd, he claimed, to see this as "one God praying to another God." Since there is only one God and Jesus is that God, any duality that we find in the New Testament must be explained as interaction between the two natures, not interaction between divine persons.

The problem, he proceeded, is that the early Christian "church" fell away from this pure faith, a faith restored in the early twentieth century in the Oneness Pentecostal movement. This ancient apostasy took place, most likely, around the time of the Roman emperor, Constantine. Constantine, for purely political purposes, embraced Christianity in name only and brought about a fundamental redefinition of Christianity as essentially *polytheistic*. The doctrine of the Trinity, he asserted, was the result of wedding together paganism and Christianity. "The Trinity doctrine is a theological monster that holds the irreconcilable claims that God is both one and three." The resultant theological "darkness" prevailed for well over a thousand years until a slow process of restoration began around the time of the Reformation. The full restoration of "truth," however, awaited the events of the early twentieth century.[‡]

---

†   Later this point will be considered more fully. Perhaps an alternative explanation of the prayers of Jesus is in order, however. Pope Benedict XVI, in discussing Jesus' prayers in the Gospel of John, notes, "Jesus' prayer is seen also by John to be the interior locus of the term 'the Son.' Of course, Jesus' prayer is different from the prayer of a creature: it is the dialogue of love within God himself—the dialogue that God *is*." Joseph Ratzinger/ Pope Benedict XVI, *Jesus of Nazareth* (New York: Doubleday, 2007), 344.

‡   Gordon Magee, author of a popular booklet in defense of Oneness theology, *Is Jesus in the Godhead or is the Godhead in Jesus?*, wrote: "The present resurgence of the truth of the full deity of Jesus is but a *rediscovery* of a very precious *apostolic* truth which for long centuries has been obscured and prevented by the Roman apostasy and its three-God theory" (18).

He then directed my attention to what he called the clearest biblical text on human salvation in the Bible: Acts 2:38. Here we find Peter telling the large crowd gathered on the day of Pentecost to do three things: (a) repent, (b) be baptized in the name of Jesus Christ for the forgiveness of sins, and (c) receive the gift of the Holy Spirit. Since we had already spoken of baptism in Jesus' name, we now focused on another subject: receiving the Holy Spirit. He asked me, "How do you *know* you have received the Holy Spirit?" "There must be an *evidence* of this experience," he reasoned. "Without a sign or evidence, one would never know if he had experienced the fullness of salvation described in the New Testament."

Indeed, upon comparing the various biblical accounts of people "receiving the Holy Spirit," accounts exclusively found in the Acts of the Apostles, one finds a recurring sign: speaking in tongues (Acts 2:4, 10:46, 19:6). What is the obvious conclusion? *Everyone* who receives the Holy Spirit *initially* speaks in tongues.

What? *Everyone* has to speak in tongues as evidence of receiving the Holy Spirit? Without this experience one cannot be sure that he is going to heaven? Of course, no verse of Scripture actually states such a thing, but the case did have some plausibility based on comparing the stories in the New Testament's Acts of the Apostles. I initially found this entirely counterintuitive, but it soon became attractive. It is not explicitly clear in the New Testament, but perhaps that is because everyone in the first century knew that first-hand and it did not need to be explicit. Perhaps it took having the experience to *see* it in the New Testament.

My conversation partner's ease in moving around the Bible was stunning. I had never met anyone that could so freely move from text to text. He must have cited or alluded to hundreds of biblical texts in our several hours together.

I later discovered that this gentleman was the evangelism minister at that church and had developed an influential Bible study that sought to demonstrate his conclusions by combining various verses of Scripture in a way that seemed to build a powerful cumulative case for his conclusions.

When my mom returned to take me home that night, I was deeply shaken. My recollection is that the most disturbing aspect of our conversation was not the series of claims presented above but the conclusion that these things are both true and *necessary for salvation*. In other words, those who are not baptized in Jesus' name and speak in tongues *are not saved*. Further, those who believe in the Trinity are not saved, either, since they worship a "false god." There was no ambiguity in his presentation. If true, the "Christians" I knew were really not Christians at all. They were adherents of a perversion of Christianity and needed salvation![†] I was immediately consumed with a desire to figure all this out and act consistently with the truth.

Over the next several months, great turmoil followed both within my own heart and mind and in my family and church. My Baptist pastor learned of my leanings toward Oneness Pentecostal theology, and he brought to my home a bag of books on related subjects. I read many of them. My father was greatly distressed by my leanings while my mom was cautiously supportive. Our family had been going through a sort of religious awakening, and my dad's attitude was more conservative and reserved, whereas my mother's was more open.

---

†   Not all Oneness Pentecostals are as insistent on this point. Some allow trinitarians the "chance" of salvation so long as they are ignorant, through no fault of their own, of the "truth." The United Pentecostal Church International (UPCI), the largest Oneness organization, speaks of their understanding of Acts 2:38 as the "Bible standard of full salvation." This leaves some room for interpreting what "full salvation" means. In my experience, most interpreted it as a minimum standard. There was no ambiguity, among virtually all those I knew, this was their position.

To make a complicated story short, my whole family land-
ed in the United Pentecostal church. There we stayed until
after I graduated from a Oneness Pentecostal Bible college in
1990. Over the seven years I was in the Oneness movement,
I gradually came to develop a more objective approach to the
subject matter as well as a broader perspective on the Bible.
Although I developed great friendships and appeared to have
a very bright future within the movement, I left within a few
weeks of graduating from the college.

This book, in large measure, is an attempt to put into
writing some of the most important ideas that led me to
leave. But it is much more than that. It is also an attempt to
explain how the arguments that compelled me to reexamine
my beliefs provided the occasion for my eventual discovery
of a much more beautiful and convincing vision of all reality. It was my discovery of the Catholic faith that brought
my meandering path to a new *fullness* that meant far more
than theological quibbling about fine points of biblical interpretation. I came to believe that Oneness Pentecostalism, for all the good that I experienced, had insurmountable
obstacles to a truly full, compelling, and enduring vision of
Christian belief and life.

Why Write Now?

I have never tried to make a "career" based on my experiences within Oneness Pentecostalism. I've got more than
enough to do with my family, my parish, and my work.
If not for a teacher's summertime reprieve, I would have
little or no time to concentrate on the present task. Back
in the days shortly after leaving the movement, I wrote
a short booklet published under the title *An Evaluation of
the Oneness Pentecostal Movement* (Pasadena, TX: Pilgrim
Publications, 1990). Although I now disagree with some

of my reasoning and see some of my arguments as insufficient, it was an early effort in writing to explain my reasons for leaving. Occasionally I have dialogued with people interested in my journey. I have sometimes mentioned my past in this movement as an introduction to describing my "conversion" to Catholicism.[†] Beyond this, most of my students and audiences through the years have no knowledge of my experience of the Oneness movement. Indeed, most of them know nothing of the movement at all.

This raises the question of why I would write on this subject now. My reasons are several. *My primary reason is that I want to help Catholics understand the beauty of their faith.* This is the task to which I regularly devote my energies. My efforts, then, are first directed toward Catholics. My hope is that the interplay between a Catholic and non-Catholic approach to Scripture and faith will provide a stimulating conversation that Catholic readers will, with heightened curiosity, eavesdrop on.

I recall a sweet Catholic couple whose faith "came alive" when they visited a Catholic bookstore. They "overheard" a Catholic employee defend his faith in conversation with a rather hostile Protestant visitor. Sometimes a contrast of perspectives creates new enthusiasm and understanding on the part of listeners to dialogue. My goal in writing, as will become apparent in the following chapters, is to develop a historically orthodox and biblically-based understanding of the Trinity, baptism, and the work of the Holy Spirit. My own development in understanding these matters was vital in preparation for my later discovery of Catholicism.

---

†   A written summary of the major reasons and experiences accounting for my conversion to Catholicism and away from Oneness Pentecostalism may be found in the Coming Home Network, November 2009, newsletter.

Second, I continue to receive requests from time to time to answer certain theological claims of the Oneness people. There are a few interesting and helpful books that have been written through the years, but none, to my knowledge, from a Catholic perspective.[†] Even those works are, despite their value, lacking in some key respects. This is especially true with respect to the issues pertaining to baptism but also to spiritual gifts. For some years I have intended to write an article or booklet on the subject of baptism and address some of those questions. It is difficult to address baptism, however, without addressing the Trinity. In the minds of most Oneness Pentecostals, Acts 2:38 presents a multifaceted experience that must be addressed as a whole. As we shall see, addressing their interpretation of that verse will necessarily include a consideration of the biblical basis for the Trinity as well as the other topics considered in this work.

Third, Oneness Pentecostals are making inroads in the world of "mainstream" Evangelicalism, especially within the Charismatic movement. There are at least some that have moved from the former days of isolationism to actively spreading the leaven of their theology in other contexts. Although these evangelists may have decreased their level of exclusivity, they still, as far as I can tell, look with disdain on the Trinity and baptism in the name of the Trinity.

Also, the Oneness movement is apparently making significant inroads in the Latin American community, both in Latin American countries and within the United States. It

---

† Carl Brumback's book, *God in Three Persons* (Cleveland, TN: Pathway Press, 1959), and Gregory Boyd's, *Oneness Pentecostals and the Trinity* (Grand Rapids, MI: Baker Book House, 1992) are the most well known full-length works. Boyd's book displays an insider's knowledge of the Oneness movement and is far superior to Brumback's. Another book, *The Trinity and Eternal Sonship of Christ* (Pasadena, TX: Pilgrim Publications, 1992), by my longtime Baptist friend, Bob L. Ross, is especially interesting with respect to his historical observations about early Pentecostal leaders.

is not uncommon, for instance, to see new churches erected or old ones purchased and the churches' new names include the word *apostolic*, typically a code word for Oneness Pentecostalism. Since most of these people are of Catholic backgrounds, their choice of this movement should be a cause of concern within the Catholic community. True to our best historical moments, we should be willing to offer a solid reply to the challenges of this movement.

Fourth, this contemporary movement, in part at least, is the reappearance of some rather ancient notions. Although I have discovered no reason to think that any identifiable group prior to the twentieth century held to all the distinctive ideas of the present movement, their notion of God, i.e., "Oneness," is an ancient one. Although it has been identified by a variety of names and subtle variations (e.g., Sabellianism, Patripassionism, Modalistic Monarchianism), the basic thesis is the same. These facts make a present examination of Oneness Pentecostal theology both historically interesting and presently relevant. Additionally, the claims of other unorthodox movements often arise from similar foundations.[†] Answering the claims of the Oneness movement goes a long way toward answering the divergent claims, for instance, of Jehovah's Witnesses, Mormons, and adherents of the conspiracy theories of books like *The Da Vinci Code*.[‡] Often we come to appreciate our beliefs more fully when they are brought into contrast with counterclaims. I hope that

---

†   By *orthodox* I mean conformity to the traditional standards of theology shared by the major Catholic, Orthodox, and Protestant creeds (e.g., Trinity, hypostatic union). The term is used primarily for its historical value, not pejoratively. I include the Protestant creeds to emphasize the degree to which the Oneness movement deviates from historical Christianity.

‡   Oneness theology is more perplexing than these other movements, however, inasmuch as it is far more Christocentric. Oneness Pentecostals affirm that Jesus is God. These facts set it apart from other non-trinitarian forms of Christianity and make it more difficult to critique, since most aberrant groups attack the divinity of Christ in some way.

Catholics and others who may read my analysis will come to a more profound appreciation of the Trinity, their baptism, and the gift of the Holy Spirit.

Although he is not a model of orthodoxy, John Stuart Mill somewhere made the point that only those who live the history of the creeds appreciate them. I've often thought of this as I try to teach theological ideas developed long ago to young people today. The most effective method I've discovered is to invite my students to relive the heresies of the past, see their appeal, and then see how and why the orthodox position eventually showed itself to be the correct one. Our minds often see best by contrasting images. Oneness theology allows us to see our faith by way of contrast and thereby, hopefully, better understand, appreciate, and believe its contents.

A significant number of Catholics have fallen into Oneness theology. I've met some of them. There is every reason to think, especially in light of the rise of Pentecostalism in Latin America, that this challenge will only grow. I hope this presentation will aid in some meaningful way in this struggle.

Fifth, this work is an act of reflection after almost three decades since leaving the United Pentecostal Church. My initial emotional attachment to the movement has long passed away. My appreciation of the history of theology and the complexities of religious experience has, I think, deepened. My ongoing study of the related topics, especially the Trinity, has only strengthened my convictions. As a Catholic, I am obligated to work for the *unity* of the Faith and believe that the entire world is called to embrace the good news of Jesus Christ, the fullness of which is found in the Catholic Church. I hope that some understanding and, perhaps, dialogue, will result from this work.

It should be emphasized that Oneness Pentecostals are a *minority* of the Pentecostal movement. The majority of the denominations that call themselves "Pentecostal," and most of those adhering to the Charismatic movement do not profess the doctrines described above. This is not to minimize the size of the movement. Although statistical information is incomplete, the movement numbers in the millions and is found in almost 150 nations throughout the world. My point, however, is that readers should not generalize about these doctrines when speaking of Pentecostalism. On the other hand, the Oneness movement does raise special questions for the rest of the Pentecostal world and, indeed, Protestant Christianity altogether. In response to these questions, I am convinced the Catholic Church has something meaningful to share.

The Plan

My plan does not include an exhaustive study of the issues involved in discussing the theological ideas mentioned here. That would require a complete systematic theology. My intention is to set out paths of thought that decisively lead us away from Oneness Pentecostal theology and toward Catholic theology, especially as these have been influential in my own intellectual and spiritual journey.

We shall begin with the subject of baptism. Chronologically, it was this issue that was presented to me first. It is also the subject that most Oneness Pentecostals feel is their strongest and most obvious position. We will then consider Oneness theology and the Trinity. This is, without doubt, the most important part of this work. The Trinity is "*the* central mystery" of the Catholic faith, according to the *Catechism of the Catholic Church*, 234. *Everything* we believe originates in that sacred mystery, even if we don't realize that fact. If God is truly a Trinity of divine Persons, all of reality has come to be because that God willed it to be. Next, we will consider the baptism of the Holy Spirit and its relationship to speaking in tongues. Although this topic is the least important in respect to its rank on the theological spectrum, it is relevant to many because of the attention it receives in certain circles. It also provides an opportunity for us to examine Pentecostal hermeneutics and present a Catholic understanding of the work of the Holy Spirit. Finally, our focus will shift to the question of why I chose to embrace Catholicism. Catholic thought is so foreign to Oneness Pentecostals that it is necessary to conclude our study with a presentation of a few of the reasons I entered the Catholic Church.†

In a real sense, this entire work explains how my study of the Bible resulted in a progressive discovery of Catholic faith. Since the mystery of the Trinity is the heart of Catholic faith, my discovery of that truth moved me progressively nearer to the Church. For those readers who might find some of the material difficult and are therefore tempted to jump ahead to another topic, I'm confident the chapters may be read with profit in any order.

Does It Really Matter?

Does it really matter if we believe in the Trinity? Most Catholics and most Oneness Pentecostals cannot fully

---

† It is not my intention to write for scholars, and therefore I will not provide footnotes for every claim I make. My hope is that this presentation will take the form of a conversation with Oneness Pentecostals (and other interested persons) that grows out of my own experience as a Oneness Pentecostal, including years of study in a United Pentecostal Bible college and relationships with many "mainline" ministers and teachers. The movement has not produced a wealth of theological literature. This accounts for some of the theological ambiguity that exists about Oneness Pentecostalism. By far the most prolific and persuasive writer in the movement is David K. Bernard (now general superintendent of the United Pentecostal Church International) whose numerous books published by Word Aflame Press (Hazelwood, Missouri) provide the primary theological presentations of their beliefs. Excluding, of course, official organizational documents and periodicals, works almost always designed for popular consumption. Bernard's books provide a fine service to the movement since they summarize the major arguments, ideas, and claims that are found throughout their churches.

articulate their beliefs on these matters, anyway. Perhaps we should conclude that what we *think* is of little importance. Maybe we should think, as many do, that Jesus was not the Son of God but a *moralist*. If we *behave* as a Christian, does it matter if we *believe* as a Christian?

It is my conviction that this attitude is entirely unacceptable and contrary to the nature of Christian faith. *What we think shapes the way we behave.* Even though an atheist may behave in ways that resemble what is expected of a Christian, he lacks a solid answer to *why* he should do so. If there is no God, no judgment, and no "objective" moral law, the reasons to behave as if there is a God dissipate. Although not as extreme, the theological differences between the topics discussed in this work have great consequences.[†] We may not understand it, but our beliefs regarding the nature of God, including the Trinity, have a wealth of practical consequences. Because these consequences become part of the fabric of faith over time, we often fail to see those links until we have abandoned them, to our peril.

Finally, if we are truly followers of *Christ*, we cannot reduce him to a moralist. Jesus was not crucified for professing a set of moral principles. He was crucified for claiming to be the *Son of God* (Mark 14:61–64). Our faith not only calls for the submission of our *will* to God but also our *mind* (Luke 10:27). We are invited to verbalize the assent of our *intellect* to truths revealed by God regarding himself every time we

---

† A former student of Oneness Pentecostal background recently sent me an email suggesting a connection between Oneness theology and a trend of "dictatorial" pastors. The Trinity affirms a God who is an eternal *communion* of love. Oneness theology, on the other hand, affirms an eternal *solitary* God. My student's experience, although it does not demonstrate a *necessary* consequence of Oneness theology, may confirm a *tendency* toward a certain view of God and, as applied especially to pastoral ministry, authority.

recite the Nicene Creed: "I believe in God the Father . . . in one Lord Jesus Christ . . . and in the Holy Spirit."

A number of years ago, a student of mine asked why we were spending so much class time trying to understand the mystery of the Trinity. He thought it was a waste of energy. He argued that we could better use our energy trying to figure out how to feed the hungry and clothe the naked rather than exploring mysteries of theology. To love others is all that is important. I replied by noting that, statistically speaking, it is likely that he will one day marry some young lady. I further suggested that his future wife might on occasion wish to tell him about her day, her likes or dislikes, hopes or dreams, experiences, etc. I instructed him to respond by saying, *"I love you, but I don't want to know about you."* He immediately saw the absurdity of his position. I then asked him to call me and tell me about her reaction. The point should be clear: *if we really love God, we will want to know what he has revealed about himself.*

1

The Baptismal Formula

"I baptize you in the name of *Jesus Christ* for the forgiveness of sins." This, we believed, was the *essential* wording for the New Testament practice of baptism. One's sins are forgiven when the name of Jesus is orally pronounced over a person being baptized, we reasoned, since the New Testament declares that salvation is found in "no other name" (Acts 4:10–12).

It is somewhat challenging to describe just how important the spoken name of Jesus is to Oneness Pentecostals. Just typing those words makes me a little uncomfortable. The name of Jesus is surely indispensably and eternally important to every Christian. It is the importance of *Jesus* to Christian believers that makes the Oneness Pentecostal emphasis on the "name" not only plausible but also potentially very attractive.

Josef Pieper's great book, *Leisure: The Basis of Culture,*† makes the case that human beings are capable of engaging in two fundamentally distinct ways of looking at life. On the one hand, life may be viewed as survival within the day-to-day

---

† This book has long intrigued me. I first learned of it many years ago from Ted Rebard, one of my beloved philosophy professors at the University of St. Thomas (Houston). He described this book as one of a small handful of books that changed his life.

flow of bodily and social needs within our temporary existence. It is not possible to go very long, for instance, without
thinking about what we will eat, how we will pay our bills,
putting gas in the car, mowing our grass, going to work, and
figuring out how to get the kids to school and back.

It is possible to become so immersed in the realm of temporary concerns that we forget that there is another plane or
perspective from which to view the world and our place in it.
For most people, there are at least some moments when they
are invited into thinking about "big" questions. Perhaps this
is when a loved one passes away or a child is born. Maybe
it happens when a person realizes they are growing old or
that the years are passing quickly. Sometimes it happens while
listening to a beautiful song or watching a moving film or
play. In such moments, a person is challenged to see life in
terms of the "big picture." How does everything fit together?
What does it all mean? Where did it all come from? Where
is it going? How should I live my life? Some people are more
regularly drawn to thinking on this level. They may be more
sensitive to art, music, a beautiful sunset, or a religious icon.

There is a danger in sensing the "iconic," however. The
age-old temptation to stop at the sign or image rather than
allowing it to lead us to that reality to which it points is
never far away. The Catholic Church has never ceased to
wrestle with this challenge, but others are not immune to it
either. Maintaining a balance between images or signs and
the realities to which they point is a challenge inherent in
the human condition.

Several years ago I drove from St. Louis to the Louisville,
Kentucky, area for the specific purpose of visiting the monastery where the well-known Trappist monk and spiritual
writer Thomas Merton lived. I had recently read a number
of Merton's books. I arrived a day early for a conference in

St. Louis and drove to the monastery. After spending some time at Merton's simple gravesite and walking around the grounds, I stopped into a bookstore and giftshop. There was a large collection of icons on several tables that caught my attention. Browsing around, I found one icon of Mary and Christ that caught my attention. It was of Greek origin, painted around the sixteenth century. The description on the back side of the icon pointed out that the direction of the eyes of Mary and Christ should be the focus of the observer. Often such icons have Mary and Christ looking at each other. This one, however, had both looking forward. The description identified this as a "Sweet Kissing style" and noted that the direction of their attention is intended to serve as an invitation to everyone looking at the icon to enter into the love that is shared between Christ and his mother. That thought so moved me that I bought the icon. After purchasing it, I found a bench outside the store, overlooking the hills around the monastery, and prayed that God would grant me a deeper share in the love that is represented by that picture. It now sits on a table near the front door of our home. Occasionally, when walking by that space, I will stop and recall that moment in Kentucky.

Icons fascinate me. Perhaps this is partly because of my Pentecostal background that had no place for images of Christ or of the saints. Our understanding of the commandment to "make no graven images" was iconoclastic. We believed it is sinful to make or make use of such images for religious purposes. In fact, my United Pentecostal pastor[†]

[†] Arless Glass, well-known United Pentecostal minister, was my pastor during my seven years in the Oneness movement. Despite our theological differences, I learned much from him. His seriousness about his beliefs, love of books, and efforts to teach me humility when my youthful energy was accompanied by too high an estimation of my abilities all have had a lasting impact.

would occasionally explain why we don't have crucifixes or even crosses in our churches. He said it was because Jesus is no longer on the cross. I always felt a little uncomfortable with this reasoning since, although it is true that Christ is no longer on the cross, remembering the cross and Christ's death are important and meaningful.

For many reasons, I later came to think very differently about our iconoclastic tendencies. For one, the Bible regularly uses imagery for God. If we think about what we are reading, we inevitably form images. The Old Testament tabernacle and, later, temple, were filled with artistic symbolism and representations. The Ark of the Covenant contained objects that were revered by the Israelites, since they reminded them of God's work among them (i.e., tablets of the Ten Commandments, Aaron's almond branch, jar of manna). If one understands the commandment against "graven images" as excluding artistic representations of religiously significant matters, surely there is much to explain in the Old Testament.

A better explanation is that the Old Testament commandment does not exclude visual imagery that stimulates the religious imagination. Instead, the commandment is warning against crassly identifying such visual imagery with the reality to which it points. Indeed, this happened in Israelite history when, for instance, the bronze serpent that reminded the people of God's healing during the time of Moses became a superstitious object revered for some inherent power it was believed to possess (2 Kings 18:4). The same object that was used to bring salvation became an object of idolatry. Interestingly, still showing the importance of God's saving action even after Israel's idolatry, Jesus uses the same bronze serpent to foreshadow his own manner of death (John 3:14).

The Incarnation of the Son of God is the supreme "icon" of the invisible God (Col. 1:15). Being a Christian is based squarely on the conviction that when we encounter Jesus, we are encountering God's presence as mediated through the real humanity of Jesus. We will later have reason to explore these claims in more detail. The Catholic Church has wrestled with the use of artistic representations of Christ and concluded that their use is not only allowable but makes an important theological statement. By allowing visual depictions of Jesus, we are continually affirming the reality of the Incarnation. God personally united himself to the real, visible, and tangible humanity of Jesus at a real moment in history. Jesus was truly God's visible self-revelation. To insist that we are not allowed to form "images" of Jesus is to insist that we not be allowed to think of his humanity. Our humanity is experienced in the world of space and time. To think of Jesus as we think of the Gospel stories requires that we form images. Artistic images can help stimulate the imagination to a true and deeper affirmation of the Incarnation. If one refuses to think of Jesus in imagery that is consistent with our real physical existence in space and time is, implicitly at least, to fall into the heresy of Docetism. According to Docetism, Jesus only *seemed* to be a man but really was only a spirit being.†

---

† For further reading on images, icons, and the importance of imagination and visual experience, see Christoph Schonborn, *God's Human Face* (San Francisco: Ignatius Press); Jeroslav Pelikan, *The Christian Tradition: A History of the Development of Doctrine, vol. 2: The Spirit of Eastern Christendom* (Chicago: University of Chicago Press, 1977); and Alister McGrath, *The Twilight of Atheism: The Rise and Fall of Disbelief in the Modern World* (Colorado Springs: Waterbrook and Multnomah, 2006). Schonborn's work focuses heavily on the iconoclastic crisis during the first millennium of the Church. Pelikan's work focuses on the development of eastern Christianity more broadly but gives significant attention to the theological issues surrounding the use of icons. McGrath's work is an insightful look at contemporary atheism, but along the way includes a fascinating analysis of the loss of the sense of the sacred alongside the renewal of iconoclasm within early Protestantism.

There is an all-important line that must be drawn between superstition and the use of images through which
we discover the realities that transcend the image-forming
power of our minds. As humans, our manner of knowing
divine realities is through or by means of things that are
infinitely less than or inferior to God. We move from the
world of finite, dependent realities to the infinite and independent reality that is God. The finite and dependent point
us to that reality upon which they depend. The constant
temptation is that we stop at the dependent things and treat
them as if they were the supreme realities. The temptation
of iconoclasm is to destroy everything that is less than God
as a path or avenue to God.[†] As tempting as that path may
be, it fatally ignores the fact that we must travel through the
creation to the Creator. God has chosen to "hide" behind
the creation and allow us to freely discover God within the
experience of his effects.

In all sincerity, my earliest memory of thinking about
God was standing in the kitchen of my grandparents and
looking at a wall. It was a beautiful wooden wall. I don't
know why it happened at that moment, but I was struck by
the question, "Why is there anything at all?" It was years
before I shared this experience with anyone, and I still hesi-
tate to do so. In that moment, I seemed to see *through* the
wall that I observed and intuitively saw that it, and every
other dependent thing, depends on that which depends on

---

†   Protestant iconoclasm inclined toward limiting the "means" of God's revelation to the
preached and written word of God. Some years ago I attended the funeral of a student
of mine who died in a car accident. The funeral was held at a large Presbyterian church.
Upon leaving, some students who attended the funeral noted that the church building
had no art, the pulpit was at the center, there were no stained glass mirrors, and the
other customary uses of the sign of the cross, genuflecting, etc., were missing. The long
practice of finding God in the beauty of the creation as well as the beauty of redemption
as displayed to all the senses in Christian worship was noticeably absent.

nothing at all. In other words, there must be a first, independent, self-existent reality that explains the dependent things that I experience in this world (myself included). We call this "first" reality God.

Katie, our youngest child and a rising sophomore in high school, recently got her first official job working at a restaurant near our home. A young man who worked at the restaurant suddenly passed away only a few days before I wrote these words. My daughter is experiencing the same challenging thoughts and emotions that we all experience when we have our first experience of losing someone who was present to us in the daily rhythm of life. Such unforgettable moments make us keenly aware of how dependent and fragile we really are.

For our purposes here, the crucial point is that the finite, dependent realities that we experience in life become signs that point to their source: an infinite, independent reality, without which none of them would exist for even a moment. I labor this point here because the Oneness Pentecostal emphasis on "the name," in my experience, was an odd combination of iconoclasm and superstition. The more I came to see these as they were, the more inclined I was to rethink our theology.

Returning to the two "planes" or ways in which we can experience the world, I have always tended to have a strong desire to live in the second mode or plane. This sometimes causes me to pay too little attention to the everyday concerns that often preoccupy human beings. My desire to think about the big questions led me to give little thought for a significant part of my young life to concerns about making money or planning for the future.

I offer these autobiographical thoughts because they are important to understanding my attraction to Oneness Pentecostalism as a young boy. I had been so captivated by the story of God's love shown in Jesus Christ, that I was willing to do what I was convinced was necessary to follow Jesus.

I still remember the night I was baptized "in Jesus' name." Later in this work I will describe that experience in more detail. Standing in a baptismal tank, the pastor announced over me that I was being baptized "in the name of Jesus Christ for the forgiveness of my sins." Sometime later I heard this explained. When Jesus instructed his disciples to be baptized "in the name of the Father, and of the Son, and of the Holy Spirit," the "name" he was pointing to was his own name. Jesus is the Father, Son, and Holy Spirit. If one sees that "revelation," he will also see why baptism in Jesus' name is so important.

I cheerfully agreed with these ideas for years. At some point, however, I began to develop some discomfort with the way that many people talked about "the name." It started to sound more like a magical formula than a way of referring to the Jesus whom we love so much. The New Testament book of Acts records the story of certain persons who were going about trying to cast out demons "in the name of the Jesus that Paul preaches" (Acts 19:13). They were unsuccessful, to say the least. Why? Because the "name" is not a magical formula. When we speak of the name, we are talking about the one who bears that name. The name we vocalize is merely sounds without faith in the one to whom the name points. I was initially attracted to Oneness Pentecostalism because of my love for Jesus but later came to question whether the name had become something else in our understanding. Had the "name" become our bronze serpent?

Strangely, the very desire I had to follow Christ that made me open to the message of Oneness Pentecostalism made me uncomfortable when I would speak with other proponents of Oneness theology about the fate of those who were not baptized "in Jesus' name." I would ask, "What if two people are baptized and they both have deep faith in Jesus but one has the name of Jesus pronounced over him and the other does not?" Most frequently my conversation partners quickly replied that a person cannot possibly have their sins forgiven if the name is not spoken over them. This question will be considered later in this chapter, but I mention it here because it was one of those questions that became a seed in my mind that grew over time. Had the name of Jesus become for us a superstitious collection of sounds rather than a way of referring to the person who saves? How could we be so sure that only we had proper baptism? How could we be so quick to insist that only those with our formula uttered over them could be confident of forgiveness?

These concerns were part of the logic that caused me to question the "Jesus' name" baptism position.

Origins of "Jesus' Name Baptism"

Virtually every other form of Christianity that has existed through the centuries has understood the baptismal formula issue very differently than what we find within Oneness Pentecostalism. Jesus commanded his disciples, shortly before his ascension into heaven, to baptize "in the name of the Father, and of the Son, and of the Holy Spirit" (Matt. 28:19). This, traditional Christianity has reasoned, is what we are supposed to say when we baptize.

The early Pentecostals, a movement born shortly after the turn of the twentieth century, baptized using the words of Matthew 28. It was only later that a new revelation was declared. Claims of *revelation* were quite common in those days. The movement was originally founded on the claim that some important truth of early Christianity had been lost. In order to rediscover that and other possible lost truths, one must be courageous enough to confront and, if necessary, discard *traditions*. In fact, as all experienced in such movements can testify, *tradition* is most often a bad word. Indeed, there are biblical texts that can be read in support of this attitude (e.g., Mark 7:13). On the other hand, the Bible speaks highly of tradition (2 Thess. 2:15). If *tradition* is understood as that which is passed along from one generation to the next, the Bible itself fits that definition. It is too simplistic, then, to simply discard everything categorized as tradition. Some tradition is good, and some is bad. The question that should concern us, then, is how can we tell the difference between them?

The original *cause* of Pentecostalism was the supposed rediscovery of the biblical observation that all who receive the Holy Spirit initially speak in other tongues. That is, they are miraculously enabled to speak in languages never studied, learned, or, most likely, even heard. God overwhelms the speaker, it is claimed, as a way of showing that the human speaker is completely under the control of God's Spirit. Alongside this experience was an attempt to recover other spiritual gifts mentioned in the New Testament but neglected by the traditional churches (e.g., healing, prophecy).

Since those who accepted the Pentecostal experience typically embraced the Trinity and an understanding of church ordinances (they didn't use the word *sacraments*) that would fit nicely in most cases with what you would learn about in a Baptist church, baptism was not a chief concern.[†] This was because (a) most had a traditional understanding that felt little need to question and (b) the ordinances were not

---

†   Some, like Charles Parham, the "founder" of Pentecostalism, were rather indifferent to water baptism altogether. See James R. Goff, Jr., *Fields White Unto Harvest* (Fayetteville, AR: University of Arkansas Press, 1988), 35.

essential to salvation and therefore were practically of little importance. That is, until a new "revelation" would shake this young movement to its core.

When John G. Scheppe ran shouting through the Pentecostal camp meeting in Los Angeles, California (1913), in the middle of the night declaring that he had found a new truth and that this truth pertained to the proper baptismal formula or wording, it was met with mixed reactions.[1] In studying the biblical book of Acts, Scheppe found that baptism was uniformly performed "in the name of Jesus." What followed was a mass of rebaptisms. Those who resisted rebaptism were considered unspiritual and entrenched in tradition. The peer pressure toward rebaptism was enormous and extended even to the highest authorities in the young movement. When the question of rebaptism turned into a denial of the Trinity, however, many in leadership grew gravely concerned. In time, the majority rejected the rebaptism teaching and professed the Trinity as the most faithful representation of the biblical teaching about God. A significant number did not, however.

To this day, informed Oneness Pentecostals are most comfortable defending their understanding of baptism "in Jesus' name." Because the baptismal formula question *caused* the birth of Oneness Pentecostalism, we will consider that topic first.

Formula?

Examining the various texts in the book of Acts (and a few elsewhere) that mention baptism "in the name of Jesus," I suggest that the first question that should come to mind is: *what does the text actually record was said at the moment of baptism?* In point of fact, the texts rarely say anything about what was said. It is, then, an *interpretation* of the texts to say they represent a formula. To make the point clearer: there is no text that says anything to the effect, "When they were baptized, Peter *said*, 'I baptize you in the name . . .'" To some this may seem trivial, but it is crucial. The point at issue is what *wording* must accompany baptism in order for it to qualify as legitimate Christian baptism.

A *formula* refers to a *precise wording* that must be spoken in order for an ordinance to be valid. To use a more Catholic way of speaking, the "formula" is what gives *form* or specific shape or significance to the material element of water. Dipping a person in water does not necessarily have a Christian meaning. A parent can give his child a bath and pour water over his head. That action is *not* New Testament baptism. The action of dipping or pouring with water must be accompanied by the proper intention and words that specify the *meaning* of the action.[†] Consider two friends in a swimming pool. One dips the other under the water. There is no reason to suppose that this is a Christian baptism. If we were observing a baptism, on the other hand, we should expect to hear words that state the purpose or meaning of that action. What wording is *required* for the action? The Oneness Pentecostal answer is that "in the name of Jesus" is the bare minimum.

As noted, though, there is no text that mentions the words spoken at the baptismal ceremony. Well, this claim should be qualified. For instance, the Ethiopian eunuch asks Philip to baptize him, and Philip replies, "If you believe with all your heart" you may be baptized (Acts

---

† Oneness Pentecostals insist on baptism by *immersion* only. Since this stance is not unique to them, however, it will not be discussed in detail here. I would argue, though, that the Greek word *baptizo* allows for a plurality of modes and the New Testament usage implies the same (compare Acts 1:4-5, 2:4, 33, 38, 8:16, 10:44-48, 19:5-6). In these texts we find a variety of descriptive terms for the "baptism with the Holy Spirit": poured out, filled, baptized, came upon, etc. The meaning of "baptism" can be expressed, then, through more than one mode.

8:37). The eunuch answers, "I believe Jesus is the Son of God."† In this case, however, it is not the administrator of baptism who makes this statement but, rather, the person receiving baptism. Further, the formula, "in the name of" does not appear. Does this suggest there was no formula? No. The author simply does not find it needful to report such a formula if it was used. What we do learn from this text is that Christian baptism is grounded in the belief that Jesus is the Son of God, a conviction that is consistent with both Acts 2:38 and Matthew 28:19. Baptism is not merely a profession of belief in "Jesus" without qualification but, rather, our faith is grounded in the Jesus who was the *Son of God*.

A second text is equally important in this context. Paul encounters some disciples of John the Baptist in the city of Ephesus (Acts 19:1–6). He asks them, "Did you receive the Holy Spirit when you believed?" They answer, "We have not heard that there is a Holy Spirit." Paul counters, "*Unto what then were you baptized?*" They say, "John's baptism." Paul explains that John's baptism pointed to Christ and then baptized them "in the name of the Lord Jesus" (v. 5). Notice again that the text relates a conversation, but the conversation ceases *before* the baptism. We are again left without explicit direction about what was said at the moment of baptism, only that it was done "in the name of the Lord Jesus," whatever that is intended to mean.

The conversation itself should be carefully examined, however. It appears that these disciples of John did not

---

† Most contemporary translations of Acts 8 exclude this verse since the oldest manuscripts conclude the conversation with the eunuch's request for baptism. Oneness Pentecostals typically accept the validity of these disputed verses, however, and so we will not engage the critical textual questions. At a bare minimum, the text represents a very early understanding of baptism, even if these words were not original.

know that the Holy Spirit was not yet available, suggesting they did not know the messianic age had dawned. Their ignorance of the Holy Spirit prompted Paul's question, "*Unto* what *then* were you baptized?" Carefully note that Paul's question is prompted by their ignorance of the Holy Spirit, indicated by the word translated as *then*. Second, note that Paul's question begins with the word *unto*. This English word is used to translate the Greek preposition *eis*. This term, one that will recur in our study from time to time, is pivotal in this context.

Prepositions in the Greek language help clarify the function of certain cases. Unlike our language, Greek nouns are formed with endings that indicate their function in a sentence. A word that functions as a direct object, for instance, will appear in the accusative case. A word functioning as the subject of the sentence will appear in the nominative form, the indirect object in the dative case, and so on. Prepositions are used in the language to clarify the exact function of these cases since some have multiple functions. The preposition *eis* suggests motion or attention directed *toward* something. Accordingly, it is variously translated, for instance, as "unto," "with reference to," "toward," and "into." Paul's question, then, has the following sense: "If you don't know about the Holy Spirit, what did your baptism *make reference to?*" The implication is that baptism *should* include reference to the Holy Spirit. Since the disciples of John at Ephesus were apparently ignorant of the Holy Spirit, Paul immediately turned attention to their baptism and what it referred to.

Since their prior baptism was related to John and his ministry, Paul now baptizes them "in (*eis*) the name of the Lord Jesus," a phrase that can easily be read as a contrast with John's baptism. Their new baptism pertained to or had reference to the name of Jesus rather than John's prophetic ministry. We will have to examine these terms more carefully as we proceed, but we have already discovered some revealing things.

Similar to the Acts 8 text concerning the Ethiopian eunuch who connected Christian baptism with a profession of Jesus as the *Son of God*, the Acts 19 text suggests that Christian baptism makes reference to the *Holy Spirit*. Both these observations are consistent with Matthew 28:19, a text that speaks of baptism "in (*eis*) the name of the Father, Son, and Holy Spirit."

Let's take one more look at this point. Compare the following baptismal texts:

- "Baptize in (*eis, with reference to*) the name of the Father . . . Son . . . Holy Spirit" (Matthew 28:19).
- "We do not know whether there is a Holy Spirit. Unto (*eis, with reference to*) what then were you baptized?" (Acts 19:3–5)

It is hard to avoid the conclusion that Paul's question to the disciples of John in Acts 19 strongly implies that Christian baptism makes reference to the Holy Spirit.

The two New Testament texts, then, that record some dialogue around the act of baptism mention a profession of Jesus as the *Son of God* and reference to the *Holy Spirit*. If the "bare minimum" of a baptismal formula, according to the Oneness Pentecostal, is "in the name of Jesus," these texts are odd indeed.

In sum, looking at those few texts that actually include a conversation or specific citation of words uttered around the moment of baptism, we find words that are consistent with the use of Matthew 28:19. Those receiving Christian baptism are expected to profess that Jesus is the Son of God and make reference to (*eis*) or have attention directed toward the Holy Spirit.

The Name

The Bible makes frequent reference to God's name. God's name is, we are told, holy and must not be used in vain. It is well known that the Jews took this so seriously that the holy name of God, YHWH, is not spoken out of fear that it would be misused. The original pronunciation of that Hebrew word is lost to history on account of their strict refusal to use the name.

It is also well known that this holy name of God is rooted in the narrative of Moses before the burning bush. Moses questions God about his "name." If Moses is to confront Pharaoh and, as God's representative, insist that he release the Hebrews from the bonds of slavery, he must know the name of the God making this demand. Further, he must know the name of the God of the Hebrews if he is to speak to the people of their God. To this request God responds, "I am who am"; and he says, "Say this to the people of Israel, I am has sent me to you" (Exod. 3:14).

A "name," if it is a good one, gives insight into that to which it refers. The name of God is so radically holy because it brings us into contact with a reality that transcends our comprehension. If the human mind pales before the holy mystery of God, how may we give a "name" to that reality? Wouldn't any name we give to God fail to capture the reality signified by it?

Surely it is not possible for us to *comprehend* the nature of God. Consequently, the Bible speaks of our inability to "see" God (e.g., John 1:18; 1 Tim. 6:16). On the other hand, some individuals are privileged to "see" God, at least in a "dark cloud" or by way of some visible appearance that God may temporarily assume, sometimes called a theophany. To complicate matters further, our heavenly hope is to "*see* God" (Matt. 5:8). If we seek to harmonize these various ideas, we are pushed to grant that, in some meaningful sense, humans have been given insight into God's nature but that this insight must be qualified as far short of a *full* grasp of the infinite God. Our hope is that the limited knowledge we now have of God will be far surpassed in the life to come. In light of these distinctions, it is possible to say some men have "seen" (i.e., partial insight) God but, at the same time, none have "seen" (i.e., full comprehension) God.

Somehow, then, our nature must either be *elevated* to "see" the God that is far too great for us to behold in our current condition, or God must *come down* to our level and communicate himself in a limited but meaningful way so that we may be able to "see" him. In light of the fact that we are unable to fully *grasp* the nature of God, the names by which God reveals himself to us will include the paradox of our desire to see him but our inability to fully do so. There is some meaningful level of knowledge available to us, although it is bathed in mystery and obscurity. We do not *comprehensively* see God, but we do know God in a limited way; albeit, as St. Thomas Aquinas liked to say, alluding to Moses' vision of God on Sinai, "in a dark cloud."[2]

The "names" by which God is revealed to us, then, either emphasize our inability to understand or they are tied to something that God does. For example, we speak of God as "Creator," a label signifying God's relationship to the world as its cause. We speak of God as "savior," a label signifying God's relationship to creatures in need of deliverance from sin and its effects. The name *Jesus*, or

Yeshua, in fact, corresponds precisely to this second meaning (literally: "Yahweh saves"). The name *Jesus* is so important in the New Testament (indeed, it is at the "name of Jesus" every knee will bow, Phil. 2:6–10) because it is in him that God is most supremely revealed to the human family. We "see" God in Christ, and therefore the name of *Jesus* stands for that highest *means* of divine revelation.

The name YHWH, assuming it should be understood in relationship to the words of God to Moses, "I am who I am," may emphasize God as *pure being*. At least this is a possible interpretation. If so, God is differentiated from all other beings inasmuch as finite beings are distinguished from others by some *limiting* way of being. For instance, since I am a man, I am not a bird. My "way of being" limits me. God, as pure, unlimited being or existence, is not limited by any restricting "essence" and therefore is an infinite ocean of reality that is ever greater than my ability to think or define. When God speaks, then, he reveals himself as, "I AM." Our understanding of God's essence reaches its limit when we admit that we lack the power to "comprehend" God. I can say, "I am a man," but not, strictly speaking, "I am." God (since all reality is a finite expression of what exists infinitely in him) cannot be defined apart from the rather vague and mysterious name, "I AM." That is, of course, with the exception of those names of God that are attached to actions of God that we can understand more directly (e.g., creation, salvation).

The key point to keep is that a name reveals, on some level, the *reality* to which it points. Christians must be careful to avoid a superstitious approach to the names of God. God's name is not holy because of the sounds or letters that make it up. Rather, it is holy because of the reality to which it refers and helps to specify.

I often got the impression that Oneness Pentecostals viewed the name of "Jesus" in a somewhat superstitious way. It is the invocation of the name of Jesus that *causes* the forgiveness of sins in baptism. The individual's faith is not the primary instrumental cause of forgiveness but, rather, saying the name of Jesus.[†] This leads to the impression that saying the name is "magical" in nature. One person may be baptized with the words of Matthew 28:19 uttered over him while another with the words of Acts 2:38. Theoretically, even though their interior faith is identical, one walks away still a sinner while the other is forgiven. The difference between whether one is saved or lost, then, depends on the words spoken over him.[‡]

From a Catholic perspective, it is true that our salvation involves others. As a social and historical creature, I receive the contents of my faith through others who have passed it along to me. In that sense, then, my salvation involves others, and it cannot be viewed as a radically private event. We also speak of "formulas" that are essential to the validity of the sacraments. Those formulas, however, are determined based on the *meaning* of the sacramental actions and express that meaning. The sacramental meaning is foremost while the formulas *safeguard* that meaning. Although a Catholic priest, for example, would not accept Oneness Pentecostal baptism as valid, this is not because it could never be the case that a baptism is effective

---

[†] I avoid raising the issue of infant baptism here. The Catholic approach would emphasize the faith of the believing community, including the infant's parents, as vital to the meaning of baptism. It is, fundamentally, an act of faith.

[‡] Bernard denies that the name *Jesus* is a magical formula or incantation. He insists that faith is essential in the person, and therefore uttering the name of Jesus alone is not sufficient (David K. Bernard, *The New Birth* (Weldon Spring, MO: Pentecostal Publishing House), 164–5. My remarks here reflect my own experience, however. Moreover, if two persons have the same faith in Jesus but one, as described above, does not obtain the forgiveness of sins, it is more than faith in Jesus that causes forgiveness.

if the words, "in the name of Jesus," were uttered.[†] Instead, the baptism is not valid for the Catholic because (a) it does not express the *full meaning* of baptism as trinitarian and (b) the Church's discipline on this matter requires the minimum of the Matthew 28:19 expression.

Also, the Catholic approach would insist that God has chosen to give the graces of salvation to human persons in and through physical signs. We are creatures that discover the spiritual world in and through the physical world. As Paul explains, the invisible things of God are known through the visible world made by him (Rom. 1:20). The forgiveness of sins is a reality that cannot, strictly speaking, be *seen*. God imparts the forgiveness of sins in association with external signs since we are not merely spiritual beings. Physical acts provide a window into those spiritual realities signified by them and become the normal means or pathways by which the spiritual realities are given to us. Baptism, then, beautifully "pictures" the forgiveness of sins in a way that we can observe, but also *imparts* the very forgiveness it pictures (Acts 2:38, 22:16, and so on.). It is not some mysterious quality of the water or words spoken, however, that causes this forgiveness. It is the power of God's Spirit that brings about the effects of the sacraments

---

†   Thomas Aquinas, for instance, interprets the texts that speak of "baptism in the name of Christ" as instances of a "special dispensation of he who did not bind his power to the sacraments" (*Summa Theologiae* III.66.6). He conjectures that an exception was allowed during the early apostolic era "in order that the name of Christ, which was hateful to Jews and Gentiles, might become an object of veneration." It is interesting that he also deals with the position that either baptism according to Matthew 28:19 or "in the name of Christ" is acceptable because the Father and Holy Spirit are implied in the name of Christ. He does not deny that such an implication exists, but he insists that the *sensible form* of the sacrament be conformed to the original elements of the sacrament as instituted by Christ. He rejects the validity of any baptism without mention of Father, Son, and Holy Spirit, since the sensible "form" of the sacrament should be conformed to Christ's baptism in which there was a sensible presence of the Father (in the voice from heaven), the Son (standing in the water), and the Holy Spirit (descending in the form of a dove).

(e.g., John 3:1–8). The new birth of water and Spirit is "from above" (John 3:31). God is its cause. In my experience, Oneness Pentecostals frequently speak about the baptismal formula in such a way that the *source* of the effects of the action resides in the utterance of the name of Jesus.

The Church does not presume to make a final judgment on the souls of persons not baptized with this formula, but it does insist on a minimal standard of meaning, and this standard is expressed in the formula.[†] The same could be said of the other sacraments. Even with respect to the Eucharist, it is the Church that, in safeguarding the meaning of that sacrament, determines what wording is essential. Sometimes this requires the invocation of the words of Christ's institution of the sacrament, but exactly how many of those words are necessary involves some flexibility, as indicated by the history of the eucharistic prayers.

Sometimes Catholics, especially schismatic ones, fall into a mentality similar to the Oneness Pentecostal in requiring a formula that can hardly be distinguished from a magical incantation. It is one thing to say that a formula is a bare minimum on account of the discipline of the Church in maintaining the correct meaning of the sacramental actions; it is another to say that the words themselves, within themselves, have the power to cause the sacramental graces. It is the power of God's Spirit accompanying the words that produces the effects. The words of Matthew 28:19 are most naturally understood as the appropriate formula for baptism

---

[†] See Thomas Aquinas, *Summa Theologiae* III.60.7-8. Aquinas cites Augustine: "The word operates in the sacraments *not because it is spoken*, i.e. not by the outward sound of the voice, *but because it is believed* in accordance with the sense of the words which is held by faith. And this sense is indeed the same for all, though the same words as to their sound be not used by all. Consequently no matter in what language this sense is expressed, the sacrament is complete." Throughout Aquinas's treatment of this and related subjects, he continually emphasizes the importance of maintaining the proper *meaning* of the sacraments in the words used. Several interesting examples are offered in III.60.8.

because (a) they are the most direct, concise, and clear words of institution of the act of Christian baptism and (b) they express the meaning of the action: baptism directs him, and therefore initiates him into, the community of people who believe in God as Father, Son, and Holy Spirit.

One final observation is in order. From what has been presented in this section, it should be clear that a name and the reality to which it refers are very closely connected in the Bible. In fact, there are many texts in which the word *name* should be equated with its object. The "name of God" is often a way of saying "God." Given the Hebrew mindset found in the Old Testament, this is quite understandable. Fear of referring to God in an irreverent way gave rise to a host of *indirect* ways of referring to God. Matthew, consistent with this tradition, consciously avoids repeating the word *God* too often and thereby offending his Jewish readers. Instead of using "kingdom of *God*" repeatedly, then, he tends to use "kingdom of heaven." God was often spoken of by way of those things closely associated with him, like "heaven". "The name" (*ha shem*) was one of those ways (e.g., Ps. 5:11, 20:1). It would be ironic indeed to take "the name" and treat it as an end in itself, since its very purpose is to reveal and direct attention to the God before whom we should rightly tremble in awe and reverence. As a consequence, even though the name *Jesus*, derived from YHWH, is pronounced in a thousand different ways throughout the world, the crucial issue is the intended meaning and reality indicated by the term, not the sounds themselves.

Names and Titles

The crux of the Oneness Pentecostal argument regarding the baptismal formula is the distinction between names and titles. I am, for instance, a father. My kids call me "Dad." I recall that when my daughter was around five years old, she struggled to come to terms with the fact that other children called their fathers "Dad." She would sometimes ask me, "What is your name?" When I told her my name is "Mark," she had a confused look on her face. She slowly came to understand that "Dad" is a common title given to men that stand in a certain relationship to children. *Mark*, however, is my proper name.

This is not the end of the confusion, however. There are others who share the name "Mark." One of these is my oldest son. While they were growing up, my younger children expressed a fair amount of confusion at the fact that two people in our home share exactly the same name! Turning to the name "Jesus," the same is true. In fact, many people shared that name in the first century, evidenced by its widespread presence on ossuaries and in contemporaneous literature. The early Christians would add other terms to the name *Jesus* in order to specify exactly who was intended (e.g., Christ, Lord). The neat distinction between names and titles is then blurred somewhat by usage.

Additionally, upon examination it is found that proper names originate as what Oneness people would call titles. The name *Jacob*, for instance, means swindler. *Esau* means reddish. *Adam* means man. *Isaac* means laughter. For those familiar with the stories about these people, all these names reveal something about their stories. I am told that my name, *Mark*, means "strong defender." None of these terms, presumably, *originated* as proper names but were first adjectives or common names.

Consequently, there is nothing to prohibit *father* (or *son*) from becoming a proper name if, by usage, it is uniquely associated with an individual. If, for instance, there is one supreme Father and all other "fathers" are only fathers in a relative or lesser sense, the word would function as a proper name in reference to God alone. Jesus affirmed as much when he said we ought not to call men "fathers" since there is only one Father, God (Matt. 23:9). Of course, this hyperbolic expression should be taken together with the rest of biblical language. Jesus himself used the word *father* to refer to human beings (e.g., Luke 15:18–29). The point of Jesus' statement is clear, however: there is only one "Father" in the fullness of what that term means.

The goal of the distinction Oneness Pentecostals make between names and titles, of course, is to argue that Father, Son, and Holy Spirit are not names but titles. The name of the Father, then, is something other than "father." If none of these terms are names, we must search for another name for use in baptism.

I happily accepted this distinction along with our interpretation of Matthew 28:19 until I discovered that the New Testament itself refutes this logic. The text that most disrupted my thoughts was Hebrews 1:4–5.

In this important text, the author writes of the glory and greatness of the *Son* in contrast to the angels. This is the central motif of the entire book: the supremacy of the Son of God above every other "medium" of divine revelation. Although God spoke in various ways "to the fathers in the prophets," he has now spoken to us "in his Son" (v. 1). After declaring the radiance and power of the Son, the author states that the Son is "much better than the angels" since he has received a "name" more excellent than any angel. In proof of this claim he cites Psalm 2:7: "You are my *Son*, today I have begotten thee." The author's point is clear: no angel is called *the* Son of God.†

---

†   There are references to, apparently, angelic beings as "sons of God", but the writer of Hebrews is basing his argument on the singular and personal nature of the Psalm 2 text ("my Son").

This name differentiates him from all others and gives him a place of dignity and supremacy that is unparalleled. The idea is not a generic use of "son" but, instead, "*the* Son." No one reading the New Testament can be mistaken about who this "Son" is, and therefore these words become a proper name, not an ambiguous title. In fact, as we shall see, there is and can only be one Son in the full and proper sense of this term.

In conversations with Oneness Pentecostals about this text, they often try to argue that the "name" in question here is actually *Jesus*. There are two apparent problems with that claim. First, the name *Jesus* is not mentioned in the immediate context of the author's argument. Second, and most importantly, the whole argument hinges on the word "Son," *not* Jesus. It is not the name *Jesus* that makes him higher than angels but, rather, the name *Son*.

I discovered, then, that the distinction between names and titles was groundless. Whether a word functions as what we would call a "title" or a proper name must be determined from contextual usage, not a predetermined set of distinctions from current English usage.† With that discovery, I could return to Matthew 28:19 and see that baptism "in the name of the Father," etc., was not a list of titles directing attention to another name but, in fact, was offering insight into the God that must be professed by all who choose to follow the way of Christ. Father, Son, and Holy Spirit are *unique* names that, when understood, cannot possibly refer to any other realities than those defined by the New Testament context.

An important issue remains. Why is the word "name"

---

† Another relevant example is the name "Abram" or "Abraham." "Mighty father" or "Father of many" as such, would not be considered proper "names" in our current usage.

singular in Matthew 28:19? Doesn't the singular suggest that
there is one name that belongs to Father, Son, and Spirit?
There are two possibilities. First, the structure of the verse
assumes the repetition of the word *name* in each phrase:
"Baptize in the name of the Father, and (*in the name*) of the
Son, and (*in the name*) of the Holy Spirit." Let's say that the
United States, Mexico, and Canada all send you as an am-
bassador to a meeting in Europe. You address the crowd: "I
have come in the name of the government of the United
States, and of Mexico, and of Canada." It would be a mis-
interpretation of your words to claim that there is a single
government of these three countries. The repetition of "the
government" is implied in the structure and intent of the
sentence. So, too, it is a mistake to construe the singular
"name" here as a reference to something other than Father,
Son, and Holy Spirit.

Second, it is possible to read the singular in a more mysterious way. Since, as already noted, the "name" of God is a
Hebraism referring to the reality of God himself, it may be
that Jesus' baptismal command indicates that baptism directs
attention to the one God who is revealed as Father, Son, and
Holy Spirit. Both the unity of being and plurality of persons
in God are brought together in the great command institut-
ing Christian baptism. In fact, this threefold baptismal expression within the framework of the firm conviction that
God is supremely one gives rise to the threefold creeds of the
Church, beginning with the Apostle's Creed. Baptism obli-
gates one, then, to belief in one God who is Father, Son, and
Holy Spirit.

"In the Name"

Does acting "in the name of" another primarily and necessarily refer to a required *formula*? Oneness Pentecostals

are so used to assuming that the answer to this question is "yes" that it is often hard to persuade them to examine their assumption.

I recall a conversation many years ago with a very fine Oneness preacher. He was a young, but sharp, mind. He was a few years behind me in the Bible college I attended. He learned that I had left the movement, and he sought me out. His goal was to persuade me of my errors and encourage me to return to the "truth." Our conversation, as was typical, focused on the baptismal formula. The Bible between us was opened to Acts 2. I asked him to provide a text that gave the exact words that were spoken at the moment of baptism. He pointed me to Acts 2:38. Over and again I insisted that the text records the command of Peter but not the words spoken at the baptism itself. I noted, as discussed earlier in this chapter, that his was an *interpretation* of the text, an interpretation I disagreed with. I couldn't seem to get through to him. He looked at me with a look of incredulity. He seemed as baffled with my inability to "see" his point as I was baffled with his inability to see mine.

The reality is that doing something "in the name of" another does not primarily refer to what he says. Colossians 3:17 is abundantly clear: "*Whatever* you do in *word* or *deed*, do all in the name of the Lord Jesus." All Christian life is supposed to be lived "in the name of the Lord Jesus." This cannot possibly mean that we audibly utter the name of Jesus every moment of our lives.

David Bernard, the most prolific theological writer of the United Pentecostal Church at this time, admits as much: "The verse (i.e., Col. 3:17) primarily means to say or do everything with the power and authority of Jesus, as his representative, as his follower, and in dependence upon him."† He goes on to argue that some actions appropriately include the oral invocation of the name of Jesus while others do not. Baptism, he reasons, is one of those that does.

The key point, however, is that doing something in the name of Jesus is not primarily a reference to the words spoken but to the authority by which the action is done. If, for instance, Jesus said to baptize while *saying,* "in the name of the Father, and of the Son, and of the Holy Spirit," *actually doing this would be a baptism "in the name of Jesus" since it is done by the authority and command of Christ.* At the expense of wearying the reader, it must be noted again: *it is an interpretation of the "Jesus' name" texts to say they speak of a verbal formula.* This interpretation is highly debatable in light of the data of Scripture and the earliest known interpretations of these texts.

It is necessary to emphasize the main point of the prior paragraph since it provides a reasonable reconciliation of the biblical texts in question. If the various texts that speak of baptism "in the name of Jesus" may be reasonably interpreted as references to the authority and power of Christ by which the action is performed, repeating the words of Christ's institution of the sacrament would be strict obedience to Christ and therefore is accurately described as a baptism "in his name."

It is worthy of note that one of the earliest Christian writings we have outside the New Testament supports this interpretation of the New Testament texts. In the early second-century work *The Teaching of the Twelve Apostles* also known as the *Didache,* we find reference to baptism "in the name

†   Bernard, *The New Birth,* 162. Bernard's words here work quite well when applied to texts commonly used to say that the "name" of the Father and the Holy Spirit is Jesus (John 5:43, 14:26). When Jesus speaks of coming "in my Father's name," this certainly is not claiming that the Father is *called* Jesus! As seen throughout John's Gospel, this refers to Christ's mission from the Father. He is sent bearing the authority and power of his Father. The same is true of the Holy Spirit, sent by the Father and Son with the mission of testifying of the Son.

of the Lord" as well as baptism "in the name of the Father, Son, and Holy Spirit."[3] The author of the work hints of no tension between the two expressions. Whenever the actual instructions for the baptismal act are given, the words of Matthew 28:19 are used, but when baptism is referenced more casually, baptism "in the name of the Lord" is used. Let's note several important points from these facts.

First, this ancient text reflects the exact situation that we find in the New Testament itself as seen in Matthew 28:19 and Acts 2:38. Second, this document interprets the words of Matthew 28:19 as the *formal words uttered* during the action of baptism. Third, no contradiction is implied in the two expressions. The most reasonable explanation is that already suggested. Baptism "in the name of the Lord" means baptizing by Christ's authority. That authority is expressed in Matthew 28:19, and therefore the words of Christ are appropriately recited at the moment of baptism.

Bernard is forced to speculate that the references to the prevailing understanding of Matthew 28:19 expressed in this early document are either interpolations (later corruptions or additions to the manuscript tradition) or reflect a stage in history when both "formulas" were accepted.[4] Our interpretation has the advantage of harmonizing the texts both in the New Testament as well as in the early historical documents outside the New Testament.† If we

---

† Nineteenth- and twentieth-century historians and theologians often found the "evolutionary theory" of religion attractive. For this reason, they frequently argued that the Trinity was far too complex to exist in the first century. As a consequence, anything in the New Testament that reflected or implied that trinitarian faith existed at the origins of Christianity must be an interpolation. Some argued that baptism was originally in the "simpler" formula ("in Jesus' name"), using the same texts that Oneness Pentecostals use in support. Oneness Pentecostals have often used these sources in support of their claims without realizing that these assertions are more a reflection of the ideologies of the nineteenth century than they are sound historical research.

are forced to claim that the ancient documents are internally contradictory, even though they include the same expressions as the New Testament, we should seriously consider whether we have correctly interpreted the meaning of the words.

Some years ago I took the time to examine the numerous references to baptism in the Christian writings of the first several centuries of the Church. What I discovered was that they uniformly reflect the same situation that we find in *The Teaching of the Twelve Apostles*. The interpretation that prevailed in early Christianity, then, was the same as that adopted here: baptism is "in the name of Jesus" insofar as it is carried out on the grounds of Christ's authority. That "authority" by which we baptize is found primarily in Matthew 28:19. Repeating Christ's command is therefore fitting and appropriate in the context of baptism.

There is another observation that is just as significant as that already made concerning the phrase, "in the name of." Whenever the Acts passages that speak of baptism "in the name of Jesus," or some other variation, are closely examined, they reveal other differences that are not trivial. It is obviously the case that the passages vary in their usage of the names/titles "Lord" and "Christ." There is another set of variations that is theologically significant.

The book of Acts (as well as the rest of the New Testament) was written in the Greek language. We are deeply grateful for the many translators of the Bible that have labored to give us the text in a language we can understand. The numerous languages into which the Bible has been translated are a testimony to the efforts of translators and the desire for the Bible throughout the world. For that we are thankful. It is nonetheless the case, however, that the work of translators is always subject to the text from which it was translated. In other words, a translation never renders the original text irrelevant.

All translations should be evaluated by how well they have communicated the sense of the original text. Since translators of the Bible are typically committed to a particular understanding of the Bible or religious tradition, their biases may be observed in their translations. Some of these biases are overt and some are subtle. Further, sometimes translators fail to capture the true sense of a text because of their ignorance of some other context that would provide a necessary background for the wording and meaning of that text.[†]

Acts 2:38, 8:16, 10:48, and 19:5 all use the words, "in the name of" Jesus Christ or Lord Jesus to describe baptism. In these four texts, however, there are three different prepositions used, all of which are translated by the single English word, *in*. The uniform use of "in" for three different Greek words obscures the variations of meaning expressed by the Greek prepositions. Acts 2:38 uses *epi*. In Acts 8:16 and 19:5, the preposition is *eis* (already discussed). Acts 10:48 uses *en*. Generally speaking, the first, *epi*, means, literally, *upon*. *Eis* means *unto*, *with reference to*, or *toward*. *En* means *within the sphere of* or *in the context of*. Although some may feel slightly intimidated by the various Greek words mentioned here, some consolation, I hope, may be found in the fact that we will need to examine only three words!

---

† Some years ago I was surprised to find the *New American Bible* translates the Greek phrase, *anthropou theou* (literally, "man of God") as "one who belongs to God" in 2 Timothy 3:16. A cursory examination of the biblical texts using the phrase "man of God" reveals it is a technical expression for a *prophet* or *divine spokesperson*. This fact seriously affects the sense of 2 Timothy 3:16, a sense that is clouded by the generic phrase chosen to translate the meaning of these words. This text brings together all inspired Scripture and the "man of God" or divinely authorized spokesperson for God in a given area: the bishop. Paul is addressing Timothy, also called "man of God" in the only other use of that phrase in the New Testament (1 Tim. 6:11).

Perhaps some illustrations will be helpful. The prepositions *epi*, *eis*, and *en* are used hundreds of times in the New
Testament. Since we cannot survey every instance of their
use, we will focus on a few uses within Luke's writings since
we are seeking to understand how he used these words.[†] In
the story of the paralytic, healed by Jesus, for instance, Luke
states that the men who carried him "went *upon* (*epi*) the
housetop" (Luke 5:19). In the same story, Jesus states that
the Son of Man has "authority *on* (*epi*) earth to forgive sins"
(v. 24). The apostles "laid hands *on* (*epi*)" the Samaritans to
impart the Holy Spirit (Acts 8:17). Beyond the sense of these
few examples, there are various shades of meaning in the
hundreds of actual uses of this preposition. Virtually all of
them, however, carry the sense of *resting upon* something or
standing in near proximity to it. The emphasis is typically
on contact and pressure exerted toward something. Baptism
"on" (*epi*) the name of Jesus, then, emphasizes the relationship of dependence into which the baptized enters through
that sacrament.

Eis, on the other hand, although bearing some similarities with *epi*, emphasizes more the movement *into* something or some place. The disciples saw Jesus go "*eis* heaven"
(Acts 1:11), and they went "*eis* an upper room" (v. 13). David prophesied of the Messiah that his soul would not be
left "*in* (*eis*)" the underworld. (Psalm 16:10) The lame man
healed by the words of Peter and John went "*eis* the temple"
praising God (Acts 3:8). The consistent sense of this word
is movement into something, often in terms of geographi-
cal motion but, in other cases, a more spiritual or figurative

---

†   Luke is the author of both the Gospel bearing his name and the book of Acts. Both
     works are addressed to Theophilus (Luke 1:3, Acts 1:1), and the second work directs
     attention back to the "first book," which dealt with the life, death, resurrection, and
     ascension of Jesus.

sense is in mind (e.g., Acts 10:48, 14:22). Baptism "into" (*eis*) the name of Jesus would suggest, then, movement from one context or state of life into a new one.

The preposition *en* carries many of the same connotations as our word *in*. It can mean "among," "within," and even "through/by," depending on the words it is associated with. Mostly it is a word that directs attention to a particular sphere of influence or meaning. Jesus, in a particular parable, speaks of a servant speaking "*in* (*en*) his heart" (Luke 12:45), and, in another text, of the "tower *in* (*en*) Siloam" (13:4). There are six days "*in* (*en*) which men ought to work" (13:14). In light of the regular use of this word, baptism "in" (*en*) the name of Jesus, although many shades of meaning may be implied, suggests that one has been placed within the sphere of Christ's influence and authority.

Imagine a square, three-dimensional figure. The preposition *eis* would signify something that is directed *toward* that figure. *Epi* would signify something sitting *on* that figure. *En* would signify something *within* the figure. All the Acts texts in view here indicate that it is the "name of Jesus" that baptism is somehow related to. If we take "name" here as indicating Christ's authority and power, we conclude that Christian baptism directs us *toward* the authority of Christ (*eis*), grounds us *upon* (*epi*), and places us *within* (*en*) the sphere of Christ's authority and power.

Thus understood, the Acts texts are richly and variously describing the meaning of Christian baptism as an action that places the baptized into a multifaceted relationship to Christ. This conclusion is strikingly similar to the various texts in the New Testament letters that pertain to baptism (e.g., Rom. 6:3–5; 1 Cor. 12:13; Col. 2:8–10; 1 Pet. 3:20–21). In those texts, for example, the baptized are united with Christ in his death and resurrection. The baptized are obligated to live "in newness of life" as a consequence of their union with Christ. This theological richness is closely connected with the diversity of baptismal expressions found in Acts.

In conclusion, rather than a uniform formula, the Acts texts are diverse. They do not fit what one would expect of a formula (a set pattern or wording). Although this observation requires some effort to look closely at the relevant biblical texts, this effort is richly rewarded. The diverse theological meanings implied in these texts point us away from a baptismal formula toward an appreciation of the dynamic and multi-dimensional relationship with Christ that we enter through baptism.

The Theological Meaning of Baptism

David Bernard, after concluding that baptism should be performed with the formula "in the name of Jesus" notes that the only practical reason why trinitarians insist on baptizing according to the wording of Matthew 28:19 is their belief in the Trinity. Bernard argues that this is not a sound justification, however, for two reasons.

First, there are trinitarians who admit baptism "in Jesus' name" is the correct formula but who also continue to believe in the Trinity. Second, the fact is, he argues, that the Trinity is unbiblical. Consequently, there are no good theological reasons for baptism in the name of the Trinity.

With respect to the first argument, those trinitarians who deny a connection between baptism and trinitarian faith are certainly standing outside the traditional understanding of baptism. In fact, the vast majority of Christian theologians through the centuries have recognized an inseparable connection between the faith of the Church and the meaning of baptism. The threefold structure of the ancient symbols or creeds certainly grew out of the ancient baptismal confession embodied in Matthew 28:19.†

Second, the claim that the Trinity is not found in Scripture is one that we will have to discuss at some length in the next chapter. For the moment, it is sufficient to recall the contents of the present chapter. Recall that Acts 8 and 19 both indicate that Christian baptism should include some awareness of Jesus as the *Son of God* and of the *Holy Spirit*. Elsewhere we find emphasis on the role of the *Father* in our salvation and baptism (Rom. 6:4). Indeed, when we do all that we do "in the name of the Lord Jesus," we are also to give thanks "through him to God the *Father*" (Col. 3:17). If giving thanks to the Father should accompany actions done in the name of the Son, and if the Son of God should be professed and the Holy Spirit recognized, we have discovered all the subjects mentioned in Matthew 28:19 outside that text. Can we seriously entertain the idea that baptism "in the name of Jesus" *must exclude* explicit reference to the Father, Son, and Holy Spirit?

In fact, one is tempted to conclude that the only substantial argument that remains in support of the Oneness Pentecostal doctrine of the baptismal formula is the theological one. If the Trinity is a false teaching and "Oneness" is correct, baptism becomes a statement of the "true" doctrine pertaining to God: *Jesus is the Father, Son, and Holy Spirit.* If this doctrine is incorrect, however, and the Trinity is a faithful representation of the scriptural depiction of God, no reason remains for using the shorter "formula" advocated by the Oneness Pentecostal.

---

† Early Christians writers like Justin Martyr provide testimony of the growing expansion of the baptismal profession of faith into early creeds. The Apostles' Creed is the classic example of this development, all of which grows from Matthew 28:19. On this point see Henri de Lubac, "A Trinitarian Creed," ch. 2 of *The Christian Faith* (San Francisco: Ignatius Press, 1986).

Matthew 28:19 records, according to the New Testament, the institution of the distinctively Christian practice of baptism. Consequently, it is the *origin* of all other Christian baptisms that follow it. It is not unreasonable, then, to cite the authority of Christ whenever baptism is administered. That authority is concretely expressed in Matthew 28:19.

It is also profitable to note that Christian faith does not stop with the historical Jesus. The Jesus who lived among us two thousand years ago uniquely and definitively revealed God to the world. This God transcends all time. Our faith is not in "Jesus only" but in the God revealed to us through Jesus Christ.† This God, we discover, is eternally *triune*. The true goal of Christian faith and life, then, is the Trinity. Jesus is the savior who restores the human family to the path that leads to the eternal life of the Trinity (John 17:21–26). Jesus is the incarnation of the eternal Son of the Father who most perfectly reveals the Father to us. It is fitting, then, that our baptism directs us beyond all history to the God in whom we will be immersed in the eternal life of love that we call heaven. Baptism certainly points to the historical Jesus but, by demanding that we acknowledge him as the Son of the Father, we also acknowledge the eternal Person who became one with us in time and space. The trinitarian baptismal statement directs us to Jesus and the God revealed through him.

The intuition of the early Pentecostals was correct, then: *baptism using the formula "in Jesus' name" is a direct assault on the belief in the Trinity.* It was not long until that assault fol-

---

†   I'm reminded of a public "debate" I once had with a Presbyterian minister. We were asked to present our respective understandings of Catholicism and Protestantism for a college world religions course. He began his opening presentation by tossing his Bible on the floor. He then made the point that the Bible is only a book; Christianity has to do with a person: Christ. Of course, I objected to his throwing the Bible on the floor since we should show respect to the means of God's revelation to us. His point is valid, however, inasmuch as the *goal* of our religion is not a book but God, revealed in Christ.

lowed the practice of Jesus' name baptism. Trinitarians need not feel uncomfortable when reading about baptism "in the name of Jesus" in the Bible, however, since this expression is reasonably understood as directing us to Christ's authority found in Matthew 28:19. The Oneness Pentecostal movement forcefully rejects the Trinity, however, in no uncertain terms. If we find that the Trinity is well founded in Scripture, our interpretation of the baptismal formula question will be decisively confirmed.

More than once I heard Pentecostal preachers say, "I'm proud to say that a Catholic priest will not accept the validity of my baptism." My study of the Bible led me to understand why the Catholic Church embraces baptism as, at its core, trinitarian. Is it possible that we had misunderstood other biblical truths? Is it possible we had erred in our evaluation of Catholic Christianity? These are questions I was forced to ask myself.

Now we will turn to the most important question considered in this book. Is the Oneness Pentecostal rejection of the Trinity well founded? Or, on the other hand, is the Trinity a faithful and accurate understanding of God based on the biblical sources? This question is of utmost important since it will impact absolutely everything else we have to say about the Christian faith. I lost many nights of sleep struggling with this question. What I discovered was far more profound and life-changing than I ever thought possible.

The Oneness of God and the Trinity

"The word *Trinity* is not even in the Bible!" "It is impossible that there are three Gods and one God at the same time!" "I never heard one preacher who believed in the Trinity get excited about that teaching." "We don't believe in three Gods, we believe in only one!" "The Trinity doctrine was created by the Catholics during the time of Constantine; before that, everyone believed in Oneness and baptism in Jesus' name."

All of these claims, and many others like them, were declared countless times during my years in Oneness Pentecostalism. When I was first exposed to the claims of "Oneness" theology, I tried to read several books on the subject of the Trinity in order to see which understanding of the Bible was most compelling. I must admit, in retrospect, that my mind was very much swayed in the direction of the Oneness movement when I began this youthful study of the Trinity. There were serious questions in my mind, but these were overcome by the confidence and overwhelming enthusiasm that Oneness preachers and believers expressed in my early years under their influence.

Years ago, after I left the Oneness movement, I became friends with a young man involved in campus ministry at a local junior college. He enrolled in a class or two at the college so he could get to know other students and then share his version of Evangelical Christian faith with them. Shortly after we became friends, a friendship grounded in our common interest in Scripture and theology, he informed me he was dating a young lady whose father was a convert to Judaism. The father was not all that excited about his daughter dating a Christian. A dialogue developed between my friend and his girlfriend's father. In time, he asked me to help him answer the various questions and challenges presented by the father.

At the beginning of our conversation, I had no doubt that he wanted to offer a compelling case for Christianity. As time went on, however, I began to sense that he was doing more than playing the "devil's advocate" in our conversations. He was becoming more and more aggressive—a sign that his *heart* was no longer in defending Christianity but had been drawn to Judaism.

Sure enough, he informed me that he was converting to Judaism and marrying his girlfriend. I learned later that he had joined the Air Force and moved away. Some years later he contacted me again. Now, with these years behind him, he was able to look back at his choice to leave Christian faith with some objectivity. He converted to Eastern Orthodoxy.

As I look back on my boyhood "infatuation" with Oneness theology, I find a similar emotional bond of attachment that formed when I first learned those ideas. This bond was only enhanced when I attended worship services at the Oneness church that were filled with emotion, upbeat music, and forceful preaching. Additionally, the people were, in general, very kind and enthusiastic about their faith. Although my Baptist church had some outstanding qualities, it seemed rather "lifeless" in contrast to what I had discovered.

I was also heralded as something of a hero for saying "yes" to the "truth." This certainly appealed to my youthful pride and confidence. Given my maturity level and this growing bond, it was almost inevitable that I would plunge myself into this newfound movement.

I have discovered that most religious "conversions," if not all of them, are not *merely* intellectual. There is also an emotional dimension. I suspect that most lifelong Pentecostals and Catholics feel a deep "bond," especially if their faith is more than nominal, with their upbringing. There is a level of familiarity and comfort that makes it very difficult to break away from this bond. Those who do convert to something else typically find deep flaws in their present faith and superior attributes in another form of religious faith. These "superior attributes" are seldom only intellectual arguments.

In our own time, however, there is an exaggerated sense of dependence on emotion in conversation about sensitive matters. "Conversation," in fact, is often little more than expressing feelings on a matter with little reason to support it. Even if reason is used, it is often waved off as another's "opinion" and not taken seriously.

My initial rejection of the Trinity was sincere. I truly accepted arguments that I thought were sound. The same sincerity, however, led me to later admit my errors of reasoning. As a young teenager, I simply did not have the grasp of the subject that was necessary to make a sound judgment.

I've often stated that one of my philosophy professors, Ed Hauser, at the Center for Thomistic Studies at the University of St. Thomas in Houston, Texas, taught me how to read. Dr. Hauser is the most impressive example of Socratic dialogue that I have come across in my life. He forced us to think. I often felt profoundly ignorant when I left his classes, but I also learned far more in his classes than was typical.

In order to finish the master's degree in philosophy, I had to independently study four philosophy writings that I had not studied in class, and then pass an oral exam on those books in front of several philosophy professors at the university. One of the books I chose was David Hume's *Treatise of Human Nature.* It is a work of hundreds of pages with many twists and turns. I was nervous about the exam since there are so many parts to the work and some of them are quite dense.

After months of preparation, I sat before three professors and discussed those four books. Dr. Hauser was responsible for questioning me on Hume's work. He asked me to open the book to the first page. He then proceeded to ask me a series of relentless questions about the first sentence in the book. That was all. When he finished, he closed the book and another professor proceeded to question me about another book.

A single sentence? I spent months working on the whole book! Hauser knew, however, that the first sentence was the key to the whole writing. Had I waded around the entire work and not realized the significance of the first sentence, he would know I missed the most important point.

Dr. Hauser and other important thinkers I've had the privilege of knowing and studying under have taught me to read carefully. They have taught me to first understand and only then engage in argument. Although harder now than ever, it is important that we sufficiently use our minds to guide and direct our emotions and passions.

It takes a great deal of effort to stand away from one's emotional attachment to a set of ideas and look at them objectively. Every religious movement has adherents that find something about that movement fulfilling; otherwise, it would not exist. It is definitely true that Oneness Pentecostalism meets religious needs for many of those who share those convictions. The same could be said, however, for

members of movements as diverse as the Jehovah's Witnesses, Mormonism, and Islam. The fact that various different
religious systems are, to some extent, "fulfilling" is not, in
itself, a justification of the whole set of ideas that constitute
those systems. We can look favorably on some of those positive features of these systems without endorsing the whole
of them. In fact, it can be argued that those positive features
make the errors of these movements all the more difficult to
overcome. Theoretically, if there is a religious faith that is,
indeed, the "fullness of truth" in this world, that religion
would, or at least could, *fully* satisfy the religious needs of
the human person. The problem, of course, is listening to
those religious truth-claims with sufficient objectivity and,
just as importantly, fully *living* that faith.

The Catholic Church claims to safeguard the fullness of
truth in this world. Proper evaluation of this claim requires
two things: (a) a powerful, compelling, and full presentation
of the Faith by Catholics and (b) a sufficient level of objectivity and openness in those who hear this presentation.
Catholics do not aid in this task when they are Catholic in
name only. The Church directs our attention to the saints
for a compelling presentation of what the Catholic faith is
supposed to achieve in a human life.† The truth-value of the
Catholic faith should be evaluated from the perspective of
those who have *fully* believed, digested, and lived its meaning. I would invite my Oneness Pentecostal friends to consider the lives of saints as diverse as Francis of Assisi, Thomas

---

† The word *saint* ("holy one") is used in the Bible to refer to all members of the churches (e.g.,
Phil. 1:1). There are other texts that speak of sainthood as our calling and therefore the *goal*
of the Christian life (1 Cor. 1:2). Catholics tend to use this word to specially refer to those
who have *completed* their journey to God and are thereby made *completely* and irrevocably
holy by God's grace. Paul (and others) use the term more flexibly to refer to those who are
growing toward holiness and those who have completed that process.

Aquinas, Augustine, Thomas More, Teresa of Avila, John of the Cross, and a host of others before quickly writing off Catholicism as a "dead" set of traditions.

Perhaps one example will suffice to make this point. About ten years after becoming a Catholic, I journeyed with some colleagues to Spain to visit sites connected with the life of St. Ignatius of Loyola. Ignatius is the sixteenth-century founder of the Society of Jesus, a prominent religious order in the Catholic Church. Also known as the Jesuits, they are well known for establishing many schools and religious institutions throughout the world. Shortly after I became a Catholic, I began teaching theology at a Jesuit school in Houston, Texas. Nearly two decades later, I continue to work in the same institution.

During my early years teaching theology at this school, I honestly knew little about the history and spirituality of the Jesuits. I knew surface details but had devoted little energy to building on that foundation. Why? I'm not sure. I had other theological interests and perhaps also a residual resistance from my Protestant upbringing to thinking too much about saints.

This all changed when I had the opportunity to visit Spain. With Ignatius's brief autobiography in hand, our group drove throughout Spain searching for key places in Ignatius's life. Beginning in Basque country, we found the Loyola Sanctuary, Ignatius's place of birth as well as the place where he recovered from the battle wounds he received in Pamplona. That painful, slow recovery was the beginning of his spiritual rebirth. Finding himself with little to occupy his mind, he reluctantly began to read the only two books in the house: Ludolph of Saxony's *Life of Christ* and *The Golden Legend*, a collection of fantastic stories about saints.

While reading these works, Ignatius, an admittedly hard-headed young man, slowly began to learn the movements of his own spirit. He began to sense a deep longing to follow Christ as his king, in contrast to his earlier romantic notions of serving an earthly king. After his recovery he journeyed toward Barcelona, stopping at Montserrat, a picturesque mountain featuring stunning views of the valleys below and a renowned basilica and Benedictine monastery. After, Ignatius made his way to a nearby small town, Manresa. There he spent much of his time in a small cave on the outskirts of the town battling his scrupulosity and painful guilt as he developed what would become the *Spiritual Exercises*, a retreat program that laid out a path for others to share in the kind of spiritual enlightenment that took place in Ignatius of Loyola during this stage of his life.

What is the *Spiritual Exercises* all about? It is about the darkness of sin. It is about the love of God that brought us into existence and God's call to us to find his love present in all things. It is about choosing to follow Christ, no matter the cost. It is about personally encountering and staying with the Jesus who loved us so much that he suffered among us and for us. It is about being with Jesus in his resurrection and ascension. In short, it is about coming into a profound, life-changing awareness of God's love and call to all who choose to open themselves to it.

As we journeyed from the Loyola House to Pamplona to Montserrat to Manresa, my heart gradually became captivated with this man who discovered Christ in such a life-altering way. After returning home, I began to experiment with the *Spiritual Exercises*. I would find quiet time to sit and ponder moments in the life of Christ, using my imagination to enter into the stories and consider the face of Christ, his words, his tone of voice, the thoughts of those walking with him, the experience of those who encountered his healing power or words of forgiveness. I spent time at the foot of the cross and in the empty tomb. A few years later I went on a seven-day silent retreat in order to have a greater taste of the profound experience that Ignatius shared with the world through the gift of the *Spiritual Exercises*.

St. Ignatius is one of numerous saints whose lives have been instrumental in showing the vast depths of the Catholic faith. Sometimes the saints show us new approaches to expressing and living out our faith. No two of us are exactly alike. The saints show the rich and diverse ways in which individuals may respond to God's love and do God's work in this world. My experience within Pentecostalism suggested a much more monolithic vision of what the Christian life was supposed to be like. Within Catholicism, I find beauty in the austere scholarship of Thomas Aquinas as well as the simple and gentle playfulness of Francis of Assisi.

Far from being a "dead" religious tradition, then, I find within Catholicism deep resources to continually challenge my own spiritual growth. I have found in St. Ignatius Loyola, for instance, a tremendous encouragement to grow in knowing, following, and loving Jesus. I wanted this as a Pentecostal and still want it now. Catholicism has not hindered or discouraged those positive longings but it has given me an endless resource for continuing my journey with the help of the great lives and teachings of the great saints.

The Attraction of "Oneness"

My choice to believe Oneness theology was, I think, based on several things. First, I was persuaded by the arguments presented to me. The case for the Jesus' name baptismal formula was compelling at that stage of my development. Also, there was a level of cogency to the attack on the Trinity. It is true that the Bible does not use the word *Trinity* or some of the other terms used to express that doctrine. The Trinity is not an easy doctrine to understand or to explain to others. In fact, it is not uncommon to find many who should know better making basic mistakes in explaining it.

I once heard the dean of a school of theology speak on Martin Buber's book, *I and Thou* (1958). This book had a profound effect on the development of personalism in the twentieth century. Buber emphasized that we are fundamentally *relational* beings and that our sense of "I" or self is developed and meaningful only in relationship to a "Thou," or another. It is not hard to see how these insights could be helpful in thinking about the relationships between the divine Persons of the Trinity. The relationship between the Father and Son found in the Gospel of John and elsewhere sounds very much like this mutual interdependence of personal subjects.

During the question period following the presentation, one person asked the professor, "Do you think Buber's work can be used as a basis for dialogue with Jews on the subject of the Trinity?" The professor, without hesitation, replied, "Of course not. Jews believe in only one God!" I cringed, as did many others in the room, evidenced by a collective groan throughout the room.

The reality, of course, is that the trinitarian faith *insists* that there is only one God. We begin our creed with those familiar words: "We believe in *one* God." This professor should have known better. The fact is, however, that there is significant confusion about the Trinity, and this makes the claims of Oneness Pentecostalism all the more attractive. Oneness theology is compelling because it is far easier to illustrate and understand than trinitarianism. For example, in my first conversation with a Oneness preacher, he stated, "I am a father, son, and husband, yet I am only one person.

The same is true with God. God is *Father* in creation, *Son* in redemption, and *Holy Spirit* in sanctification, but only one person." This illustration is, without doubt, easy to explain and understand. In fact, I've seen its equivalent in Catholic religion textbooks!

Of course, I am neither my own father nor my own son. That I am a father implies another person: my son. That I am a son implies another person: my father. That I am both a father and a son only highlights the fact that I stand in relationship to *another* as son and *another* as father. The illusion of the comparison is that one can be father and son simultaneously without implying other persons that make those relational terms meaningful. The New Testament frequently uses the terms *Father* and *Son* to highlight an interpersonal relationship between the two. For example, Jesus states, "No one *knows* the Son except the Father," and vice-versa (Matt. 11:27). Here *mutual knowledge* is specified as part of what constitutes the unique relationship that exists between the Father and the Son. Oneness Pentecostals often attempt to define these terms as indicating relationships between God and creation ("Father in creation, Son in redemption"). This simply will not do in numerous instances. Despite the failure of the comparison, however, it is used to great effect in supporting the claim that the Trinity is nonsensical whereas Oneness theology is entirely reasonable and simple.

Returning to my reasons for embracing Oneness theology, a second reason, I must confess, is that I was intrigued by the *newness* and *freshness* of these ideas. I was drawn to the idea that most of "Christendom" had fallen away from the "truth" and I could participate in restoring that truth to the world. Being one of the few that held the precious original truths of Christianity was attractive. Through my years as a Oneness Pentecostal, I would pride myself on every "novel" theological idea

I could muster, all with the conviction that I was participating in rediscovering the original meaning of Christian faith.

In time, this second reason for embracing Oneness theology would fade and then become increasing unattractive. Over and again, I found that the "novel" ideas that I developed were really not impressive at all. I found there were good reasons why my interpretations and theories had been rejected through the centuries, and I became increasingly aware of the fact that I was engaged in a futile attempt to "reinvent the wheel." Instead of learning from those who came before me, I was acting as if I was the first to study the Bible.

My youthful pride began to give way to a measured appreciation for tradition. By "tradition" I mean the ideas and insights into the meaning of Christian faith that have been handed along through the centuries. Church history became more interesting, especially direct contact with the writings of the earliest Christians outside the New Testament. Seeing Christian faith through the eyes of those whose lives overlapped the apostles or other important Christians opened a whole new world to me. I did not, of course, slavishly submit to every word they wrote. Rather, my own thoughts were informed by humbly listening to those theological laborers through the centuries. Such dependence on those who have come before us is essential in every discipline; why not, I thought, in the disciplines that pertain to our faith? I also found that the truly meaningful insights I had and shared with others were those learned from others, typically from those who lived long ago.

Since the Oneness movement was, by historical standards, in its infancy, I began experiencing a kind of historical loneliness. The restorationist view of Church history, one in which "true" Christianity was lost for most of history, became less appealing. Add to this loneliness my discovery that honest people could read the same Bible I read and come to very different conclusions; it is quite understandable that what followed was a stage of real crisis. Although I had a fair amount of youthful pride, I was honest enough with myself to know that there have always been theologians and biblical scholars much more knowledgeable than myself. How could I be so sure of *my* interpretation of the Bible when other honest readers of Scripture rejected my interpretation?

These growing concerns would find their center of gravity in the Trinity. If the dogma of the Trinity results from a true and faithful interpretation of Scripture, the rest of our theology, I discovered, would unravel. My focus, then, beginning with my second year of college, would be the subject of the Trinity. By the time I graduated, I was firmly convinced that the Trinity is founded upon Scripture and that Oneness theology, in the face of the New Testament, requires a "forced" interpretation of the Bible that is little different from fitting a square peg in a round hole.

My initial enthusiasm about Oneness Pentecostalism waned, primarily for theological reasons. It is also the case, however, that I discovered the Oneness movement is made up of human beings. Just like any movement or church, Oneness people struggle with sins of every sort. I found all the human foibles there that one finds anywhere else. I do not discredit the movement for this reason. The oft-quoted statement is true everywhere: "If a perfect church exists, we would destroy it by joining it." My primary point is that my original enthusiasm was followed by a new sobriety in the face of human weakness, including my own. It was this realism about the human condition that gave me sufficient impetus to step back and look more objectively at my interpretation of the Bible and, more generally, my understanding of Christianity. Without doubt, the Catholic Church, too, has a lot of problems, as do all other communities. In my own journey, I made the hard choice to leave the comfort of my chosen religious profession in search of the original under-standing of Christian faith. This search would lead me, in time, to the Catholic Church.

In what follows, I will discuss some of the major claims and arguments offered by Oneness Pentecostals in support of their rejection of the Trinity. My intention is not only to answer these arguments but to also develop a biblical theol-ogy of the Trinity along the way. I have chosen to discuss the claims that are most frequently made since they provide the foundation for the other arguments that I will not ad-dress here.

We will begin (a) with the charge that the Trinity is demonstrably unbiblical because it is expressed primarily using unbiblical terminology; then (b) we will consider the Oneness Pentecostal claim that the Father, Son, and Holy Spirit are modes or roles that God assumes in time, not persons; and (c) we will consider the charge that trinitari-anism is hopelessly on a collision course with monotheism and is, despite claims to the contrary, polytheistic. After answering this claim, (d) we will briefly consider a practi-cal concern: how do we pray to and worship a God that is three persons? Much of Oneness theology centers on its explanation of the two natures of Christ: divine and hu-man. We will then (e) consider the Oneness understand-ing of the two natures of Jesus and show it is incompatible with the biblical depiction of Christ. This is followed by a defense of (f) the eternal generation of the Son of God and (g) the distinct personhood of the Holy Spirit. We will conclude this chapter by considering the related questions: (h) Does the Trinity make sense? And (i) of what practical value is the Trinity?

"Unbiblical" Terminology

"The word *Trinity* is not in the Bible!" This assertion was often made in such a way that it was expected to elicit shock and amazement from those who accepted the Trinity as a true biblical doctrine. The same observation was made concerning a host of other terms.

It did not take me long to realize, however, that we were consistently guilty of the same charge. Oneness Pentecostals, for instance, speak of the two natures of Christ. Bernard claims that Jesus "had a *complete* human nature and a *complete* divine nature."[5] On the same page he explains, "We know that he (Jesus) acted and spoke from one *role* or the other, but we also know that the two natures were not actually separated in him." This random sampling, a sampling that can be extended indefinitely, features key terms that are not found in Scripture. The Bible does not use the word *complete* to describe the natures of Christ, nor do I recall the word *role* used to describe the function of the two natures of Christ in relationship to each other (or in any other related context). I'm sure Bernard would offer a defense of these terms from the Bible. That begs the question, however. The question at issue is whether any term can be used to speak about God that is not found *as such* in the Bible.

In reality, both the trinitarian and the Oneness Pentecostal use nonbiblical terminology to try to express their respective understandings of what the Bible is saying. This use of extra-biblical terminology is a consequence of the nature of Scripture itself, and should not be used as an argument against either position. I do not fault Bernard or any other Oneness Pentecostal merely for using the terms mentioned above. I disagree with their interpretation of Scripture, but that is another matter.

Anyone familiar with the various biblical books knows that much of the Bible is in the form of *historical narrative.* A large part of the Bible is a collection of stories! Genesis is a great example of this fact, but time would fail us to survey the numerous other historical texts of both testaments. There is also a good number of biblical books, especially in the New Testament, that address a variety of theological concerns in a more direct way. Even these, however, are conditioned by their historical context and do not necessarily offer direct answers to questions that arose later. *Whether we like it or not, then, the Bible is not arranged in the form of a systematic theology book.* The books constituting the Bible primarily tell the story of God's involvement in human history, culminating in the incarnation, life, death, and resurrection of Christ. Readers are forced to systematize the contents of Scripture in an attempt to find harmony and unity of meaning. Failure to do so leaves the Bible as an unformed "mass." The moment one brings some parts of the Bible into conversation with its other parts, the mind of the reader must organize and interpret.

Those texts also prompt questions in the minds of their readers. Even though Genesis chapters two and three, for instance, never *directly* refer to human freedom, we legitimately *infer* freedom from the flow of the story. Even though Genesis 1:1ff does not directly mention creation *ex nihilo* ("out of nothing"), we infer as much from the fact that God precedes and "makes" the chaotic matter that is ordered by God's creative word. The key point is that the Bible's stories and its more didactic portions raise questions that may not have been the direct concern of the original writers, but they do *indirectly* address such questions. It is the task of those who read the Bible to draw out those meanings and then develop a consistent understanding of all those inferences that become the positive affirmations of theology. Although the Bible does not use the terminology of theological discourse (e.g., omnipresence, omnipotence, aseity, original sin), the Bible is the basis of that terminology. If the biblical basis for these terms is insufficient, they are, in the course of history, subjected to a rigorous critique and discarded.

The alternative to this procedure, of course, is to refuse to draw out the implications of Scripture into an explicit theology. Some choose this route either because they fear being unfaithful to the Bible or because they believe that the Bible cannot address future questions since they do not belong to the "author's original intent." For those who believe the primary author of Scripture is God, the second reason is unacceptable. Scripture's divine inspiration is sufficient to justify using the Bible's stories and teachings to answer questions that arose later as God's people sought to understand more fully what *must be true* in order to explain what the Bible affirms.[6] Concerning the first choice, such people often betray their own method, especially when they disagree with others. It is simply necessary to talk about the *meaning* of the Bible, and that will require the development of a vocabulary suitable to that task.

These observations suggest another important point. As already noted, the Bible does not offer a systematic presentation of theological ideas. That is not to say that there are no systematic portions of Scripture. The book of Romans is, for instance, a very ordered presentation of Paul's theology of justification and related issues. The book raises numerous questions, however, so that most interpreters feel it necessary to consult Paul's other writings, not to mention other biblical texts, to make his full intentions clear. With respect to the nature of God, however, there is no biblical treatise that systematically takes up that topic. We must organize and harmonize all the data of Scripture. The result of this procedure is increasing clarity about the nature of the God *indirectly* known by his actions. Those actions, however, carry with them a meaning that allows for legitimate inference leading to a more formal theology.

John Henry Cardinal Newman noted that a religion made entirely of propositions to which believers must assent, but not seek to understand, is a religion *that will die.*[†] This is because the human mind incessantly seeks to understand. We do not want a religion, on the deepest and most pure level, that is fully comprehended by our minds. Such would make us superior to the religion. Instead, we want a faith that surpasses our powers—that is, a religion that ever draws from us a sense of mystery and transcendence. The Bible is not merely a series of theological propositions; it is a beautiful story. That beautiful story reveals a cast of characters, the main character being God. That God is enshrouded in mystery but there are glimpses of insight that shine through the darkness of mystery that allow some measure of understanding. It is such insights that theologians seek to express in their formulations. *Indeed, in light of these insights, we are justified in drawing the conclusion that God intended his people to draw out the full meaning of Scripture through ongoing reflection on the riches implied within its pages.*

A further implication is that Church history should reflect a growing and deepening understanding of the Bible. *It is simply not possible that any one person or generation fully grasps the riches of the biblical message.* Oneness Pentecostals

---

† Early in his work *An Essay on the Development of Christian Doctrine* (1845), Newman insightfully describes the way the mind encounters a truth and then "develops" its meaning. "If Christianity is a fact, and impresses an idea of itself on our minds and is a subject matter of exercises of the reason, that idea will in course of time expand into a multitude of ideas, and aspects of ideas, connected and harmonious with one another, and in themselves determinate and immutable, as is the objective fact itself which is thus represented" (55).

often fault Catholics and others who speak of the "development" of the Trinity in history. *"Development,"* in this context, is typically understood solely in terms of *change.* If the Trinity *developed*, then it must be the case that it *did not exist* before it developed. This is patently false. Life is filled with development. The small child develops into an adult. One's understanding of numbers develops into the various mathematical disciplines. So it is with the contents of faith. Surely all reflective Christians can see that their understanding and experience of the Christian faith and its meaning grow through the years. Cessation of development either suggests that one knows everything, is stagnant, or is dead! Development is not the same as novelty. The Trinity was implicit in Christian faith, we will soon show, from the very beginning. It developed insofar as followers of Christ progressively penetrated the full significance of the words and meaning of Christ. A development, I might add, that is never finished on account of the fact that we shall never fully comprehend the infinite mystery of God.

The word *Trinity*, and all the other related terms, is shorthand for a mystery *implied* in the biblical story. The Bible affirms that there is only one God (Deut. 6:4). This God, however, is revealed in connection with the life of Jesus as a father in relationship to a son (Mark 14:36). The Son of God, Jesus, spoke of ascending to his Father and, together, they would send the Holy Spirit (John 14:26, 15:26). The Son and Holy Spirit, however, cannot be *separated* from the Father. The Son wills to do only his Father's will (John 5:30, 6:38). Everything he has comes from the Father, including his life (5:26). In light of the New Testament, it is simply impossible to imagine the Son without his relationship to his Father. The Holy Spirit, too, wills only to speak of the Son (16:13). He proceeds from the Father and is sent by the

Son. All of this language cries out for formulation. Trinitarians insist that the three relationships implied in these biblical texts simply cannot be reduced to a single, solitary person. They demand a plurality of relationships. The Son cannot be reduced to the Father nor can the Holy Spirit be reduced to the Father, and the Son.

The problem, however, is that the Bible affirms the Father, Son, and Holy Spirit are each God (John 1:1, 14, Acts 5:3–5, Heb. 1:8). If the Bible is faithfully communicating truth about God, then, the one God must exist in a oneness of interpersonal relationships: Father, Son, and Holy Spirit are the one God.

What of the term *person*?[†] We distinguish, in our experience of the world, between *things* and *persons*. It is awkward, for instance, to speak of a frog as a "person." We do not refer, except in jest, to our cars as *persons*; they are *things*. What is it that we possess as humans that is lacking in a car or a frog? In short, we are capable of loving and knowing other persons, facts that allow for community and a kind of relationship and experience that is not present among the lower animals. Augustine somewhere commented that parrots can speak words but, unlike humans, they do not understand them. This unique aspect of our way of existing expresses itself in the word *I*. We are aware of ourselves *as selves* in contrast to and in relationship to other persons. We may also be

---

† The use of the term *person* in reference to the Father, Son, and Spirit has a long history. The Latin word *persona* originally signified a mask worn by an actor in a play. It came to be used as a legal term for an individual human being. The Greeks used *hypostasis* to express a roughly similar notion. Shades of difference in meaning and usage resulted in a variety of complex controversies during the early Christian centuries. Early theologians used *persona* primarily to speak of the individuality of the divine persons in contrast to the common essence (*substantia*) possessed by each. For a helpful discussion, see Richard A. Muller, *Dictionary of Latin and Greek Theological Terms* (Grand Rapids, MI: Baker Publishing House, 1985), 223-227.

thought of as *things*, but this usage requires that we abstract from our personhood. We are certainly offended when others treat us as nothing but a commodity for use rather than *persons* who should be respected and loved.

In respect to the biblical notions of Father, Son, and Holy Spirit, is it most fitting to refer to these as "things" or "persons"? Given the depictions of each in the Bible, is it most appropriate to speak of the Father, Son or Spirit as *it* or as *he*? It is striking that the term *love* is not only applied to each of these but also characterizes the relationship *between* them (John 17:23–24). Further, the Father, Son, and Holy Spirit each speak of themselves as "I" (Matt. 3:17; John 11:41–42; Acts 13:2). In light of these facts, is it really credible to deny the use of the term *person* in reference to the Father, or the Son, or the Holy Spirit? We must certainly purify this term of human limitations that cannot be transferred to God; but the truth that God is a personal reality in contrast to a "thing" or mere "force" is, without doubt, rooted in Scripture.

The terms used to express the Trinity *are* grounded in Scripture. One may deny that it is a correct interpretation of the biblical data, but it is unhelpful to argue from the absence of interpretive terminology. Our focus, rather, should be on the biblical justification for the terminology. Indeed, I discovered that the biblical justification was quite strong.

Modes and Roles

Oneness Pentecostals frequently use the words "roles" and "modes" in their explanations of the biblical terms Father, Son, and Holy Spirit. Since they profess to believe the Bible is God's word, it is not possible to refuse the use of these terms. The issue, then, becomes their meaning. Rather than seeing them as personal names of three who are God, Oneness theology insists they are *roles* or *functions* of God in relationship to his Creation. Bernard succinctly states this claim:

> The Bible speaks of Father, Son, and Holy Ghost as different manifestations, roles, modes, titles, attributes, relationships to man, or functions of the one God, but it does not refer to Father, Son, and Holy Ghost as three persons, personalities, wills, minds, or Gods.[7]

I would like to focus on Bernard's words "relationships to man." This is a key claim. Reference to God as *Father* speaks primarily of his act of creation. *Son* refers primarily to God's actions in regard to saving human beings from sin and judgment. *Holy Spirit* primarily refers to God's activity in making human persons holy. These three "titles," then, identify functions of God but not inherent, internal *relations* in God.[†] In fact, Oneness Pentecostals argue that these roles are neither exhaustive of such divine functions nor are they eternal.[8] It is admitted that Father, Son, and Holy Spirit do have a special place of prominence, but there are numerous other "functions" or roles that God performs in the course of history. In other words, there is nothing particularly special or exclusive about the Father, Son, and Holy Spirit. One could speak of various other relationships or roles that God has toward the world.

It is worth noting that the practice of substituting the words "Creator, Redeemer, and Sanctifier" for the

---

† *Relation* signifies two or more things that have some connection to each other. This may be true of impersonal things (a book sitting on desk) or personal things (a mother's son). The Father and Son are in relation to each other, then, since they act toward each other in various ways. In our experience, relations typically exist when there are individual beings that stand in some proximity to each other. Thomas Aquinas will reason that the Father, Son, and Holy Spirit are *pure* relations since the divine Persons of the Trinity are not separate substances but do act toward each other.

86

traditional "Father, Son, and Holy Spirit" is remarkably reminiscent of Oneness theology. Ironically, Oneness people have not chosen to adopt the common use of such revised phrases, primarily because they quickly turn to the name *Jesus* rather than make use of, as they perceive them, titles. Certain brands of feminism often choose the terms "Creator" and "Redeemer" rather than Father and Son since they believe the latter are only descriptive of divine functions in relationship to the creation. In their effort to "purify" Christianity of patriarchal concepts, they substitute more gender-neutral terms.

By this act, however, they discard trinitarianism and adopt, at least practically, modalism. Father, Son, and Spirit, in this view, are divine functions *toward the creation*, not *internal* relations between divine persons. A mere functional interpretation of these terms treats the personal dimensions as relative. The function of a "father" as creator is certainly descriptive of something he does, but who could say it truly captures the full meaning of *father* as a personal being?

If Father, Son, and Spirit are ways of referring to God's "relationships to man," it follows that before and apart from the creation they have no real significance. God cannot be given these titles or functions throughout eternity but only in respect to his actions in time. They cannot be seen as granting windows of insight into the essence of God. Here were find the real crux of the difference between the Trinity and Oneness.

The Trinity is, at its core, a belief about what God is *internally*. Only secondarily does the Trinity address God's relationship to the creation. It may be that we discover the Trinity through God's actions in time, but these actions only disclose something that is more foundational: God's eternal, internal life.† To make the matter clearer: *God is Father, Son, and Holy Spirit whether or not there was ever a creation.* Oneness theology fundamentally denies this claim. Its claim is that God's *eternal* life is not revealed to us. Rather, God's temporal actions alone are revealed. It is illicit, they insist, to infer eternal relationships within God from what we see, for instance, in the relationship between the Father and Son during the life of Jesus; hence, the use of the words "modes" and "roles." These terms suggest temporary activities. If an actor performs a "role" in a play, the conclusion of the play signals a return to "normal" life. God's actions in his Creation, it is claimed, are *assumed* in time but do not reveal his eternal life.

John 17:5

This dispute, of course, can only be settled by considering what Scripture has to say on the matter. Scripture led me away from the mere *functional* interpretation of the terms in question. A number of texts could be cited in this regard, but the one that most bothered me was John 17:5. Here Jesus, while addressing his Father, refers to the "glory that I had *with* you *before the world was.*" Later in the same chapter, Jesus, still addressing the Father, makes reference to the Father's love for him "*before* the foundation of the world" (v. 24). The Greek preposition translated "with" in 17:5 is *para.* The word simply

---

† The distinction between God's triune functions in time and his eternal triune, interior relationships is traditionally expressed by the terms *economic* and *immanent.* The economic trinity is God as known in the context of Creation and, especially, redemption, whereas the immanent trinity speaks of the interior, eternal relationships within God. Although it is true that we know the immanent trinity only within the context of the economic, the terms should not be equated, as Karl Rahner suggested in a controversial essay. "The Trinity of the economy of salvation *is* the immanent Trinity and vice versa" (Karl Rahner, *Theological Investigations*, vol. 4 (New York: Crossroads 1966), 87. The Trinity affirms that if God had never chosen to create the world, he would still be triune.

means one is *alongside* another. Since the Son is addressing the Father and refers to the glory he shared *with* the Father before creation, it is most natural to draw the conclusion that the personal relationship expressed in that moment of time refers to a relationship that is eternal. This text alone is sufficient to undermine the claim that the terms Father and Son are only functional, and therefore meaningful only in relationship to the creation. *Before* the worlds were made, the Son was *with* the Father, existing in a relationship of mutual love.

Bernard answers this text (and others like it) in a way that becomes a standard appeal in similar cases. He first reduces the pre-incarnate Son to a "plan" or idea in the Father's mind: "Jesus spoke of the glory he had as God in the beginning and the glory the Son had *in the plan and mind of God.*"[9] This response substitutes the preposition "in" for "with." *Para*, unfortunate for Oneness theology, does not mean *in*; the word means "alongside." Examination of the many uses of this preposition in the New Testament (and elsewhere) reveals this consistent sense.[†] Further, Jesus speaks here as a self, a person, an "I." Is it compelling to suggest that Jesus is longing to return to "glory" as an intended "plan"? The choice of words here is simply incompatible with this suggestion. If it is better to exist as a "plan" than as a *realized* plan, we must wonder why God ever created the world!

Bernard's second argument is that this text "*could not mean that Jesus pre-existed with glory as the Son,*" since he was praying.[10] Prayer is a human act, not a divine one. Reading Bernard's explanations of this text and others like it gives the impression that he is imposing a set of axioms or assumptions on the biblical texts that force their conformity despite their

---

[†]   In fact, whenever personal subjects were in view, I have found in no exception to this meaning.

natural sense. He first lays out his understanding of God, his oneness and attributes, and then imposes that framework on the rest of Scripture, including the many texts that do not "seem" to fit his framework. The interpretations are often forced and awkward, but they are all justified by the claim that these texts cannot mean what they *seem* to mean since they contradict the previously established axioms. One should question whether this established "grid" was not set up too quickly.

Bernard assumes that "prayer" is incompatible with the apparent sense of John 17:5, and therefore an alternative explanation must be sought. He is caught in a strange situation, however, since Jesus obviously speaks about divine glory and yet distinguishes his experience of that glory from the Father's. Bernard covers both these facts by saying that Jesus longed for return to his glory "as God," but also to the glory he had as God's plan. For Bernard, two basically different "glories" are in view. This is needless and unjustified. The Son's glory with the Father must be divine glory. Placing himself *alongside* the Father supports the *divinity* of both Father and Son. The "plan" of God, however, cannot be equated with God. Elsewhere Bernard will place God's eternal love for Jesus in the same category as God's love for the Church.[†] If both God's Son and the Church are parts of the divine "plan," why is one equated with divine preexistent glory and the other is not? Is the Church "God" since it is part of God's eternal purposes and, using Bernard's logic, "with" God in his plan before the worlds were made?

If we grant that the Father and Son stand in an eternal relationship toward each other, a relationship characterized by love, communication between them is a given. That the Son

---

†   Bernard, *The Oneness of God*, 186: "He loved that plan from the beginning. He loved that future Son *just as* he loved all of us from the beginning of time" (emphasis added).

of God in his incarnate humanity expresses himself toward the Father in prayer is not a contradiction but is, rather, what we would expect if such a relationship truly exists. Surely there are features of Jesus' prayers that arise from his human nature, but the fundamental union that exists between the Father and Son is the root of that communication. The prayers of Jesus in time, in the context of his human journey, reveal a life of communion and love that infinitely transcend his immediate human context. John 17:5, and other similar texts, display, by their bursts of insight into the eternal life of God, this infinite transcendence.

John 1:1

There are numerous other texts, scattered throughout the New Testament, that speak of the preexistence of Christ prior to his earthly existence. Often the descriptions of this preexistent state feature a strong distinction between the Son and the Father.

John 1:1 is, perhaps, the most frequently cited text that establishes this point. The "Word," clearly a reference to the Son of God before the Incarnation, was "with" God before the creation of the world and yet, at the same time, the Word *is* God. Trinitarians see this as an affirmation of both the divinity of the Son of God as well as his distinction from the Father *before* the creation.

My Oneness pastor often explained this text by asking: "Who is your God?" If you answered, "The Trinity," he then read John 1:1, inserting the words "the Trinity" each time the word "God" appears. The verse then reads, "In the beginning was the Word, and the Word was with the Trinity, and *the Word was the Trinity.*" This reading is problematic for trinitarians since it suggests the Word is something *other than* or outside of the Trinity, yet, at the same time, identical to the Trinity.

If we say, on the other hand, that the Word (or Son) was with the *Father*, thereby interpreting the first use of "God" as a reference to the Father, he then suggested the following: "In the beginning was the Word, and the Word was with the Father, and *the Word was the Father.*" Here again this way of reading the text poses problems for a trinitarian understanding of it. A text that initially appeared supportive of the Trinity now poses some perplexing problems. The Oneness solution is that the Word is simply an aspect of God, the divine plan or thought, and therefore can be said, rather poetically, to be *with* God but, at the same time, is, as an aspect of God, God.

To answer this challenge and discover the true sense of John's words, we must look a bit more carefully at these words. In the first line of John's Gospel, we are introduced to the "Word," a name clearly referring to the Son of God (Gr. *Logos*, see v. 14, 18). John uses this term since it brings to mind language as the medium of communication. It is by our words that we communicate what is in our minds and hearts to others. The term also emphasizes the inseparability of a mind and the words that proceed from it. It is quite possible, as this text reveals, to *distinguish* the Father and Son but impossible to *separate* them. John's Gospel emphasizes that God has spoken his mind and heart to the world through his Son. His Son is uniquely qualified for this task since he perfectly and fully reveals what the Father is like. In fact, in "seeing" the Son, one sees the Father (John 14:9–12). This is because, as Jesus explains, he is "in" the Father and the Father "in" him. It is important to note that Jesus does not claim to *be* the Father but he does claim to stand in such a close interrelationship with the Father that he can fully represent the Father to the world. The terms *Father* and *Son* suggest that the Son originates in the Father, an idea present throughout John's writings, and fully reveals him.

John 1:1 states that the Word existed in the beginning. This implies that the Word is eternal, since he is already present at the beginning of the universe—a universe made "by him." We are further informed that the Word was "with God." The Greek word translated *with* (*pros*) suggests intimacy, or as some translate it, "face to face." Whether this is necessary is debatable. What is not debatable is the fact that the word indicates that the Word should be differentiated from the one he is with. It is also important to note that the Greek text places a definite article before God (*ton theon*), suggesting a specific personal reference. In light of the rest of the Gospel, considered with John's first letter, this is the author's way of referring to the Father (e.g., 1 John 1:2). The Oneness interpretation of John 1:1 mentioned above does not take note of these facts. Again, John provides a grammatical clue both in this text as well as 1 John 1:2 that explains why the Word is not identical with the Father.

Finally, the verse states, "the Word was God." Actually, a better translation would be, "the Word was God!" The exclamation point is appropriate since the Greek text places the word "God" first, thereby stressing the divinity of the Word.[11] In other words, though the Word was with God (or, the Father), the Word is not excluded from the sphere or realm of deity. Since the last use of "God" in the Greek text of this verse excludes the definite article, the Word is not *identical* with the Father but, instead, is *alongside* the Father.

Bernard represents the standard Oneness interpretation of John 1:1 when he understands it as teaching that God's "plan" was with him in the beginning.[12] One may rightly argue that this interpretation must weaken the sense of the word *with* in this text alongside the strong emphasis on the conclusion that the Word is God himself. Also, the trinitarian reads John 1:1 in light of the rest of the Gospel. The use of "Word" in John's prologue is a metaphor offering a suggestive image for what will be explained in the rest of the Gospel of John. Although the metaphor is not used again in the Gospel after the prologue, God's revelation of himself to the world through his Son is the key theme running through its pages. The idea here is that the way in which God is made known to the world is by his "Word." We communicate our thoughts through words. Our thoughts become physical or sensory when we put them into spoken words. God's thoughts become known to us when they are incarnated in Jesus. But it happens to be the case that God's revelation of himself is not less than God himself. Jesus is God dwelling among us (John 1:1, 1:14). God's Word that became incarnate is always alongside or "with" the Father and, in time, reveals the Father since he has always been the Father's self-revelation.

We are justified, then, in reading John's prologue in support of the belief that the Son existed with the Father from all eternity and, in time, revealed the heart of the Father since, as the Father's "Word," he was uniquely qualified to do so.

Philippians 2:6–11

Let us consider a second key text that is relevant to how we understand the relationship between the Father and the Son. Before proceeding, however, we should review the state of our study. The claim that the terms Father, Son, and Holy Spirit are merely functional and refer only to temporal divine acts is false. John 1:1 and 17:5 both distinguish between the Father and Son (or God and his Word) in such a way that we are led to affirm the reality of these distinctions *prior to* and apart from creation. The original meaning of these terms is found in the relationship they express *toward each other*, not the creation. The term *Father* directs our attention to a Son. The term *Word* leads us to question its origin or source (since words do not stand alone but imply a speaker). These are relational terms but not ones directed toward the creation. Of course, I am not denying that the Father, Son, and Holy Spirit act toward the creation. Nor am I denying that they each have unique roles in God's self-revelation. It may indeed be the case that the Father is specially associated with creation, the Son with redemption, etc. These temporal "missions" of the divine persons, however, are extensions and expressions of the eternal relations between them and are, therefore, subordinate to them. In other words, if not for the eternal relations in God, there would be no temporal missions that reveal God to us in our finite world. If there is not a Father, there would have been no creation. If there was not a Son, there would not have been the sending of the Son from the Father. If there was not a Holy Spirit, there would be no sending of the Holy Spirit from the Father and the Son (John 14:26, 15:26).

Philippians 2:6–11 is an especially interesting passage from the writings of the Apostle Paul. There is general agreement that this text is actually an ancient hymn that Paul has incorporated into his writing. If this is true, the contents of the hymn direct attention to the general faith of the early Christian churches rather than, as some might suggest, the esoteric remarks of one subtle mind.

Paul encouraged the Philippians to conduct themselves humbly and with self-giving love (Phil. 2:3–4). As was his custom, he offers Christ as the supreme example of such humility. He then explains how it is that Christ serves as our supreme example. The general flow of the argument is as follows: (a) Christ existed in the "form of God" but (b) did not cling to "equality" with God; (c) he "emptied himself" by assuming the form of a servant and the appearance of a man; (d) he humbled himself to the point of death; and (e) was exalted by being raised from the dead and given the highest name by the Father.

This rich text has attracted much attention. Despite its complexities, the general flow of the text is straightforward. First, there is a contrast in the verse between Christ's existence in the "form of God" and his assumption of the "form of a servant" and the "likeness of man." The word translated *form* in these phrases is the Greek word *morphe*. This word emphasizes the *essence* of something. Here Paul speaks of the existence of Christ as God (*morphe theou*) and his choice to take on the form of a servant and the appearance of a man. The concept here is ostensibly the Incarnation. The one who existed in the very nature of God (an affirmation of Christ's divinity) assumed a human form. This choice to adopt the form of a servant and the likeness of a man stands as the supreme act of condescension. Our choice to "humble ourselves" and become a servant to another pales in contrast to Christ's humiliation. The question we are supposed to ask is: if Christ humbled himself from existing in the glory of God himself, how much more should I be willing to humble myself?

There are other complexities in this text that we cannot explore. For instance, in what sense did the humbled Christ not "cling to" equality with God? In what sense did he "empty" himself? The standard explanation is that Christ did not cling to equality with God insofar as he gave up the external glories that were rightfully his. He veiled his heavenly glory beneath the lowly appearance of a man. He neither ceased to be God nor were the divine perfections disrupted.

Some years ago I was asked to participate in a public debate on the Trinity with a Oneness minister. I focused heavily

on this text in our discussion. I insisted that the sequence of
events in this text was crucial to its proper interpretation. The
one who was in the form of God took the form of servant and
was made in the likeness of men. The movement from divine
glory was followed by taking the human form. So understood, the text poses significant problems for Oneness theology. The one who is "in the form of God" (or has the divine
nature) is distinguished from the Father who exalts him. The
expression "form of God" differentiates the pre-incarnate Jesus from the Father but also puts him in the category of the
divine "form." After the debate, one of those in the audience
asked if I would participate in a public discussion with him on
the same topic. He said that he could offer a better explanation of Philippians 2:6–10. I agreed to participate. When we
actually did meet for that discussion, I was surprised to find
that his explanation was no better than what we had heard
in the prior debate. This convinced me that this text is of
particular importance in establishing Paul's agreement with
John's description of the relationship between the Father and
Son. Although their terminology differs, the concepts they
are communicating are the same.

Paul, consistent with John's Gospel, affirms the preexistence of Christ as God. The Incarnation is not the beginning
of his existence but a voluntary humbling of himself for the
salvation of the world. Although the term *Son* is not used in
this text, the point is the same. The one in the "form of God,"
the person of Jesus before the Incarnation, is distinct from
"God the Father" (Phil. 2:11). This distinction is not limited
to the incarnate state but precedes it.

We conclude, then, that Father and Son, although revealed to us in the course of salvation history, ultimately
refer to interior relationships within God that exist prior
to the creation of anything else. They are "relationships"

because the words used to describe them are relational terms. They are "internal" since each is identified as God. The Word (Son) is with God and is God. Jesus, prior to the Incarnation, is in the "form of God". We will show later in this chapter that the same kind of relational distinction should be said of the Holy Spirit.

One God vs. Three Gods?

Without doubt, the central concern of Oneness Pentecostals is that they believe and protect the belief that there is only one God. The doctrine of the Trinity is viewed as, at a minimum, a compromise of that truth. Authors like Bernard cannot help but characterize trinitarian belief as polytheism, evidenced by his consistent use of the plural "gods" in reference to the Trinity. In fact, Bernard suggests that a "major reason" Jews have rejected Christianity is because of the "perceived distortion of the monotheistic message."[13]

The power and persuasiveness of the Holy Bible, including both testaments, certainly includes and, in a certain sense, grows out of its *monotheism*. The book of Genesis begins with the striking words, "In the beginning God created the heavens and the earth." The picture found there is of a God that completely and radically transcends this world of changing things we call the universe. The pagan religions surrounding the ancient Israelites invariably professed gods that were tied to physical forces. This tie between gods and forces was so great that we may conclude that the gods were, at root, personifications of the cycles and powers of nature. The Israelites constantly struggled, especially during the ages of the judges, prophets, and kings, with Baal worship. The Baal deities, a family of fertility gods, were believed to control nature's forces. Sacrifices and rituals offered to these gods were believed to benefit future crops, healthy childbirths, etc. In order to placate these gods, however, it was necessary at times to sacrifice small children and engage in ritual acts celebrating and appeasing them. These ritual acts were often characterized by drunkenness and orgy activity. Although the names of the gods vary, this same pattern of fertility cults and nature religions may be demonstrated throughout the ancient world.

The Israelites were firmly forbidden to worship such gods or engage in their rituals. What reason is given in support of this prohibition? The God of Israel is not one of many gods but is the only true God. Also, Israel's God transcends the world. From this truth, three striking consequences follow: (a) God depends on nothing in this world, (b) everything in this world radically depends on this God, and (c) God is utterly unique. God cannot be reduced to or likened, in any perfect way, to anything in this world. The first commandment forbade "making graven images" of God. This commandment is a necessary consequence of God's radical uniqueness. Making a "graven image" implies that one ties God too closely to some aspect of the created order. Idolatry is precisely the failure to maintain the infinite distance between creator and creation.[†] This infinite distance can be bridged only by God's initiative in coming down to our level in the Incarnation. Even so, our knowledge of God is always characterized by darkness. Paul's words come to mind: "we see in a mirror dimly" (1 Cor. 13:12).

[†] It should be noted that the commandment against "images" was not absolute. Since humans discover God by way of the creation (Rom. 1:20), we cannot help but make comparisons between God and creatures and, from these comparisons, draw analogous similarities. The Old Testament includes numerous visual images of God in its poetic literature (e.g., God is a rock, bird, strong tower). The commandment mentioned above forbids tying God so closely to any of these images that God is reduced to a finite object from his infinity. The New Testament offers Christ as the "*image* of the invisible God" (Col. 1:15). The command against images does not exclude God's own chosen self-image: Christ.

It is of utmost importance to emphasize that Israel's monotheism was not unique merely because it denied existence to the gods of its neighbors. Its monotheism was radically unique and revolutionary because of the *nature* of its God. Israel's God cannot be fully understood by the human mind. He is absolutely unique, "one of a kind." Some went so far in emphasizing God's uniqueness and transcendence that they denied any propositions could be formulated that truly "capture" the essence of this God. The gap between the human mind and the divine mind is so great that we cannot hope to affirm anything more than the radical uniqueness of Israel's God. One thinks of Plotinus's (205–270) supreme principle: the One. The One, he argued, stands above all distinction. The mind, in order to function, must make distinctions. The One cannot be an object of thought, then. If one uses his mind to grasp the One, he has already failed. The One can be reached only through mystical experience, by union, not by thought.

Of course, this line of thought does not exclude the possibility that God is a Trinity of divine Persons. In fact, one could easily argue that, since God transcends our logical categories, both unity and plurality may simultaneously exist in a way that transcends thought. One medieval philosopher argued that contradictions cease to be contradictions when magnified to infinity. For example, the continuous curved line constituting a geometrical circle becomes a straight line when magnified to infinity. The larger a circle, the less curved the line. If the circle is infinite, the curve in the line disappears, or so it was said.[14]

None of these arguments are necessary, however, since it can be shown that there is no contradiction in affirming that God is both one and three. Nor is it persuasive to claim that belief in the Trinity compromises the uniqueness of God. The doctrine of the Trinity does not claim there are three "separate" gods or beings but, rather, there is only one supreme God. Within this one God there are three personal relations, relations characterized by love. These three relations, because they are inseparable, do not direct attention away from the one God that we discover in the Old Testament; instead, they increase the uniqueness and mystery of this God by revealing that he is not a solitary *one* but an eternal, inseparable communion of love. Indeed, one can argue that Oneness Pentecostals have failed to truly appreciate God's uniqueness or oneness by refusing to acknowledge that "oneness" in reference to God may transcend the meaning of this term when applied to human persons. To use an analogy that will be mentioned again, perhaps the interior relation in our minds between mind and thought, inseparable but distinguishable aspects of our single minds, yields two eternal, personal, but inseparable relations when magnified to infinity. (The present chapter will conclude with an analysis of this analogy.)

In order to correctly understand trinitarian belief, it is imperative that we discard all images of God as "three people" walking about or sitting in a heavenly conference room. The relationship implied in these images is far too loose to be helpful. We shall later consider some analogies for the Trinity but presently we should try our best to purify our concepts by recalling that God is "spirit" and not flesh (John 4:24). God made the material world but is not a part of it. The Incarnation features the union of God with his Creation, but we should not think in these terms when we address the *eternal* existence of God apart from the creation.

The history of Christian theology is a long, not always successful, balancing act of the truths given to us in Scripture. Some interpreters have so emphasized the *threeness* of God that it is hard to see how they can speak of God's oneness as anything more than a loose association. Others so emphasize God's oneness that the plurality of persons indicated in Scripture is abandoned. Trinitarian theology seeks to avoid both tritheism and modalism by bringing these two truths into a true harmony that compromises neither of them.

One *God*

Perhaps we should slow down a bit and carefully consider the term *one.* What do we mean when we say that something is "one"? We typically use this term to refer to a unity of some sort. For instance, I have a pile of books to my right. There are about eight books in that pile. I could truthfully say, "I have *one* pile of books by my computer monitor." I can also truthfully say that I am sitting in *one* chair. If I ask, which is *more* one, the pile of books or the chair? The best answer would be the chair. It is easier for me to destroy the pile of books (requiring only the slight movement of my hand) than to destroy the unity of the chair in which I am sitting. The unity or oneness of a rock, however, exceeds that of the chair in which I am sitting because it is more difficult to destroy the rock's unity.

When we actually stop and think about it, there is nothing in this world that is *absolutely* one in the sense that we cannot make any distinctions or differentiations within it.† My Bible sitting on my left, for instance, is made of pages. Those pages are made of paper, a composite substance. Those more basic substances composing the paper are made of smaller particles and those of smaller particles still. At the end of this investigation scientists conclude to the undifferentiated, amorphous

---

† Excluding, of course, abstractions like numbers. Aristotle's explanation of numbers as abstract quantity, leaving behind the substantial entity from which the units or numbers were abstracted, is persuasive. Numbers, then, do not exist *in themselves* but only in minds capable of abstraction.

notion of "energy." As soon as one leaves this theoretical, non-conceptual level, he must immediately return to the world of things consisting of multiple principles. Composition of principles does not eliminate our ability to use the term "one" for things, however. The use of the term *one* allows for the identification of a particular unit, whatever it is that composes that unit. You are one being. You are made of countless parts, though. Since those parts are organically united and, at least if the goal is to live, they do not exist apart from each other, we speak of them as *one*.

When we affirm that God is *supremely* one, then, we are claiming that God, above everything else, is *inseparable* and *indivisible*. Unlike God, everything else is composed of multiple principles, principles that can, at least theoretically, be divided.[†] God, however, is eternally and inseparably all that he is.

Let us assume, then, that within the essence of God there are three eternal "persons" or relationships: Father, Son, and Holy Spirit. In order to continue affirming that God is truly one, it must be the case that the Father, Son, and Holy Spirit cannot be separated from each other. Everything other than God is *relatively* one insofar as its oneness can end. The Bible, for instance, says that a man and woman leave father and mother and become "one flesh." Their unity or oneness, though, can be destroyed by death. This oneness is relative to the earthly lives of the spouses. God's oneness, however, is not relative to external circumstances, since it belongs to God to exist eternally and unchangeably in his perfections. Since God is immutable, it follows that the union of divine persons cannot be disrupted.

---

† For an extended discussion of this point see St. Thomas Aquinas, *Summa Theologiae* I.11.1-4.

Contrary to the attacks on trinitarians by Oneness Pentecostals, then, we do affirm the oneness of God. *Whatever constitutes the essence of God is absolutely and unalterably one; God cannot be divided or separated.* If the Bible affirms there are three within this inseparable reality we call God, we conclude that these three cannot be divided but, since the Bible teaches us as much, we must distinguish them in order to affirm and embrace the truth that God has revealed about himself for the sake of our salvation. Distinction is not the same as separation or division. I can distinguish, for instance, between my thoughts and will, but I cannot separate them without destroying them.

We may, then, with a straight face, profess the ancient Creed: "I believe in one God."

Prayer to the Trinity?

How do we worship and pray to a God that is actually three persons? Should we equally distribute our prayers between the three? If we spend more time addressing one in prayer and worship than another, will the others be offended? Practical questions like these are often raised by curious Oneness Pentecostals. Gordon Magee, for instance, in his list of "Unanswerable Difficulties of Trinitarianism," argues that Jesus taught the Father is the "sole object of worship." He then asks, "Will our trinitarian friends explain why Christ denied worship to the other two divine Persons?"[15]

The answer to these questions is rather simple. If the Father, Son, and Holy Spirit are truly inseparable and exist in supreme union, my prayers to the Father cannot possibly exclude, at least by implication, the Son and Holy Spirit. If I am thinking of my address to the Father *in exclusion* of the Son and Spirit, I am not praying as a trinitarian. Further, the Holy Spirit directs us to the Son (John 16:13–14). The

Son reveals the Father (John 17:6). We pray to the Father, through the Son, by the power of the Spirit (Eph. 2:18). The act of prayer itself is trinitarian inasmuch as we cannot truly pray as Christians without the sense that God is wooing us internally (Spirit), on the basis of the saving work of God's Son, to the Father. Quantifying our prayers so as not to offend one or another of the divine persons only exhibits a misunderstanding of the Trinity. Recall John's words: "Whoever confesses the Son has the Father *also* . . . whoever loves the Father loves the one born of him" (1 John 2:23, 5:1). If our prayer to the Father, for instance, is not accompanied by the sense that the Father is in eternal union with the Son and Spirit, our notion of *Father* is insufficient.

Also, if the internal life of God is characterized most supremely by *love*, it is impossible to imagine envy between the divine persons. Recall that Jesus characterized his relationship to the Father as one of love: "You (Father) loved me before the foundation of the world" (John 17:24). Elsewhere, John writes, "God is love" (1 John 4:16). Given that Jesus continually speaks of *love* as the willingness to give one's self for and to another, it is striking that God is identified with this term. One is led to question, if God *is* love, can he ever be thought of as a *solitary* person? In any case, since the essence of God is self-giving love, it is inconceivable that the divine persons envy one another, and it is also inconceivable that an act of devotion directed toward one of the divine persons could detract or stand in opposition to another. To love the Father is to love his Son and Spirit.

The Dual Nature of Christ

The "key" to the Oneness Pentecostal interpretation of Scripture, especially the New Testament, is the dual nature of Christ. Magee calls it the "great key,"[16] while Bernard writes,

When we see a plural (especially a duality) used in reference to Jesus, we must think of the humanity and divinity of Jesus Christ. There is a real duality, but it is a distinction between Spirit and flesh, not a distinction of persons in God.[17]

Those familiar with Oneness theology certainly recognize this principle as the primary one used whenever any text is encountered that seems to present a plurality in reference to God.

I recall a conversation with a Oneness friend many years ago during which I expressed some of my concerns about our theology. Although I still professed those beliefs, I was beginning to doubt them. I probably focused on John 17:5. My friend appealed to the distinction between divinity and humanity. I explained that the text refers to the glory that the Son had with the Father *before creation*, therefore before his assumption of a human nature. He never seemed to grasp the force of the argument. He was so deeply trained to think that all plurality is adequately explained using this principle that I couldn't seem to get him to consider the point I was making.

When we find Jesus distinguishing himself from the Father, we are supposed to see this as a distinction between the human nature of Jesus and his divinity. The divine nature of Jesus is none other than the Father, while his human nature is the Son. The prayers of Jesus, for instance, are explained as communication between his two natures rather than between two divine persons.

This principle seems to work, on a certain level, since most of what we know of the Son of God comes through the mouth of Jesus during his public ministry—hence, after assuming a human nature. That is, of course, with the exception of those texts affirming the existence of the Son before the Incarnation. Since we have already considered some of those texts, we will focus here on whether the Oneness interpretation of the earthly ministry of Jesus is adequate.

The Oneness understanding of the two natures of Christ sounds strangely similar to an ancient heresy: Nestorianism. Nestorius was a fifth-century patriarch of Constantinople who refused to speak of Mary as the "Mother of God" (*theotokos*). He acknowledged Mary as "Mother of *Christ*," however. His argument was somewhat compelling. Mary did not *cause* the divine nature of Jesus, but she did participate in giving Christ his human nature. Hence, Mary was *not* the Mother of God but she was the Mother of Christ. The Church rejected Nestorius's views at the Council of Ephesus (431). The reason for this rejection was that Nestorius's approach had the consequence of dividing Christ into two persons. Although it is obvious that Mary did not cause the divine nature to exist, it is nonetheless true that the *person* of Christ was none other than the eternal Son of God. The Son of God was personally united with the human nature of Jesus in the Incarnation and therefore the person born of Mary was God himself. She is the mother of God inasmuch as God is born into this world in incarnate form through her. She is not, of course, the originator of the divine nature.

Although there has been much debate in recent times over whether Nestorius would have admitted to the belief that Jesus was two persons, that conclusion did seem to be a consequence of his view. At the very least, a wedge was driven between the divine and human natures that could develop into a radical separation of natures. Oneness Pentecostalism is, in fact, an expression of that radical separation.

Bernard mentions Nestorianism when discussing the two natures of Christ. In fact, he shows some sympathy for this theory when he uses a common metaphor to explain the relationship between the natures: "One way to explain the human and divine in Christ is to say he was God living in a human house."[18] The orthodox view, however, is that there is a much greater personal union of natures in Christ than can be expressed in the image of a person (God) living in a house (human nature).

It is easy to show that Jesus, as described in the Gospels, displayed characteristics of both a human nature and a divine nature. On the one hand, we find Jesus being born of a woman, growing, learning, sleeping, growing weary, thirsting, hungering, lacking knowledge, suffering, and dying. All of these belong to a human way of existing in this world. If we understand "nature" as indicating *what* something is, we must conclude that Jesus was indeed a man.

On the other hand, Jesus says and does various things that arise from something more than a human nature. He forgives sins, casts out demons, heals the sick, calms storms, raises the dead, all by his own power. Jesus speaks in such a way that he places himself in a superior position to Moses, the great lawgiver of the Old Testament (Matt. 5:27–28). In a more explicit text, Jesus identifies himself with the "I am" (YHWH) of the Old Testament (John 8:58). The case for both the divinity and humanity of Jesus, then, is very strong. On this point we can agree with our Oneness friends.

The similarities cease at this point, however. The Oneness view interprets this evidence for two natures in Christ as support for what is essentially a two-person view of Christ. The two natures of Jesus have all the defining characteristics of persons. The human nature clearly can say "I" and the divine nature does the same. There are two "I's" or centers of consciousness and awareness in Christ, according to Oneness theology. The bond between them is much weaker than in traditional theology. In fact, there is little difference between the Oneness view and a house in which *two persons* dwell.† When Jesus states, for instance, "I am not *alone*, because the Father is *with* me" (John 16:32), this must mean that both the human person of Jesus and the divine (Father) abide together to the extent that each can speak of the other as "another" (John 5:32). Jesus even speaks of his Father as a "second witness" to himself, clearly an allusion to the Old Testament principle that multiple witnesses are necessary to prove a claim in a court of law. If the Father and Son are two witnesses, if they speak to and of the other, distinguish between themselves, etc., we are left with little choice than to conclude either that (a) Jesus is *two* persons, or (b) Jesus is *not* the Father. Since the second option is unacceptable for Oneness theology, refuge must be found in the first.

What are the grounds for claiming that Jesus is the Father? Bernard offers two standard biblical arguments. First, the prophet Isaiah identifies the Messiah as the "everlasting *Father*" (Isa. 9:6). Second, John 10:30 records Christ's words: "I and my Father are *one*." Bernard interprets this oneness as an identity of the two. Both of these, however, are awkward and forced interpretations.

The "everlasting Father" of Isaiah 9:6 is best understood as a reference to God as "alone possessing eternity."[19] Clearly the term *father* is used in various senses, even when used of God. The intended point is not to identify the Son of God with the one he will call his "Father" while he lives on

---

† The Bible college professor that had the greatest impact on my personal development during those years (Kelsey Griffin) illustrated our understanding of Jesus' conscious life by drawing a picture of a human head and drew two circles inside the head. These, he explained, represent the divine and human natures. I objected after class that this loose association of natures did not seem to fit with John's words: "The Word *became* flesh and dwelt among us." (John 1:14) These words suggest a much more profound union of God with human nature. To my surprise, he expressed appreciation and concern at my observation.

this earth. These ideas are nowhere indicated in the context. Most commentators give the sense of the words as "Father of Eternity" or "Originator Of All Ages." These descriptions apply to God generally and do not pertain to the meaning of the term Father *in relationship to* Son that we find in the New Testament.

Contextually, John 10:30 certainly uses the terminology of Father and Son and is therefore more appropriate in regard to our question. The problem here is interpreting the word *one* as identity. Jesus nowhere says, "I *am* the Father." Instead, he unites himself with the Father but in no way identifies himself as the Father. The term "one" should be taken with other similar contexts in John's Gospel. In John 17:21ff, Jesus prays that his disciples "may all be one; even as you, Father, are in me, and I in you, that they also may be in us . . . *that they may be perfect in unity.*" To be sure, the union of love that exists between the Father and Son far transcends that which exists among the people of God, but it serves as our supreme model of oneness. John 10:30, then, speaks of the union of love, purpose, and nature that exists between the Father and Son. What it does *not* indicate, however, is that Jesus and the Father are identical as persons.

Bernard also cites a few other texts that he thinks support his identification of Jesus with the Father. Hebrews 1:4 states that Jesus has received "by inheritance" a more excellent name than the angels. Bernard asks, "What name did he receive by inheritance from the Father?"[20] What answer does he give? The Son received the name "Father." This is contextually unacceptable. In our treatment of the baptismal formula, it was noted that the context of this verse stresses the name "Son" as the grounds of the superiority of the Son to the angels. Also, the "inheritance" mentioned here speaks of all that belongs to the Son by virtue of his relationship to the Father. Just as a son in a household stands higher in rank than servants, so the Son of God "inherits" the full authority and power of his Father's kingdom. Since he is "Son," in the full sense of that term, he has inherited a name greater than all others. Inheritance does not mean he has the identical name but that what he has received from the Father gives him a "name" and status that reflect a corresponding position of authority.

John 5:43 states that Jesus came in his "Father's name." The name *Jesus*, it is claimed, must be the name of the Father. Thus, we have an identity between Jesus and the Father. Again, this conclusion simply does not follow. One cannot read the context of these words and conclude that Jesus is claiming to be the Father. To come "in the name of Jesus" certainly does not mean we are identical with Jesus. We are to do all we do "in the name of Jesus" (Col. 3:17). Does this mean our name is "Jesus"? If we do things in the name of Jesus, we do them in his power and authority, in obedience to his commands. Jesus came "in his Father's name" inasmuch as he came by his Father's will, desiring to accomplish it. In other words, Jesus denies that he has come in opposition to the will of God; he has come fully resigned to do the will of his Father. His whole life is an expression of his determination and willingness to do God's will.

While speaking to his apostles, Jesus stated, "He who receives you receives *me*, and he who receives me receives him who sent me" (Matt. 10:40). The structure of this verse requires that we distinguish between the apostles and Christ as well as between Christ and his Father, the one sending him. Oneness theologians tend to interpret expressions like that found in the second half of this verse as support for an identity between Father and Son while ignoring the consequences of this approach if applied to the first half. If the first part of the verse means that Christ is the Father, the second part means the apostle *is* Christ!

We are constrained to the conclusion, then, that there is no good biblical reason to support the notion that the Son of God is identical with the Father. Scripture definitely supports a profound union between them but certainly not an identity. This conclusion does not mean Oneness theology has been totally discredited, but it does mean that one of the most important links in their system is undermined. Oneness Pentecostals know full well that, practically speaking, their central emphasis is on the *identity* of Jesus with the one God. That one God is *one person*. If it can be shown that Jesus is the Father, and therefore both Father and Son simultaneously, their position is strengthened significantly. This cannot be done, however.

We must return to our point of departure, then. *Jesus does not claim to be the Father.* Is it best to interpret the texts that refer to the Father and Son as references to the divinity and humanity of Jesus? We must answer no for two solid reasons.

First, the consciousness of Jesus as revealed in the New Testament is always a unity. We fail to find, for instance, references to the Son of God *from the standpoint of the Father* that come from the mouth of Jesus. We find countless references to the Father from the mouth of Jesus but nowhere do we find statements from Jesus *as the Father* regarding the Son. Those statements expressing divinity do not include reference to the Son as distinct from himself (e.g., John 10:30). The words of Jesus are sufficient to affirm (a) he is the Son of the Father and (b) he is God, but they are *not* sufficient to affirm he is the Father. I ask again: *where is an unambiguous text where Jesus speaks of himself as the Father in contrast to the Son?*

Numerous texts can be offered for the reverse formulation: "I am not alone, for my Father is with me . . . I came forth from the Father . . . I will pray to the Father," etc. Do the Gospels ever record words of Jesus indicating, "I am not alone, for my *Son* is with me . . . I sent forth my *Son* . . . my *Son* will pray to me." These suggestions seem foolish but only because we know, by familiarity with the Gospels, that Jesus consistently speaks as Son, not as Father. Even when he makes claims of divinity, these never contradict this rule. *The most natural reading of the Gospels, then, confirms that Jesus claims to be the Son of the Father, distinct from him and yet possessing the same divine nature.* This common divinity, somehow, does not detract from or dissolve the distinct reality of the Father from the Son.

Second, the Oneness understanding of the natures of Christ fails in view of those many texts that speak of Christ's existence prior to the Incarnation (e.g., John 1:1–18, 17:5; Phil. 2:6–10). Since these were discussed above, I'll not repeat those texts. Their importance cannot be minimized, however.

The importance of this section must be emphasized yet again. Because this principle is considered *the* key to interpreting problematic texts regarding, especially, the Father and Son in the Bible, its failure strikes at the foundation of the revised modalism expressed in modern Oneness Pentecostalism.

Begotten Son or Eternal Son?

Oneness theology rejects the notion of an "eternal Son" and uses the biblical words "begotten Son" as its primary basis for that rejection. After presenting a definition of the term *begotten*, Bernard reasons,

> There must be a time when the begetter exists and the begotten is not yet in existence, and there must be a point

in time when the act of begetting occurs. Otherwise the word *begotten* has no meaning.[21]

His conclusion is that the words "Son" and "begotten" are contradictory when used with the word *eternal*. The notion of an *eternally* begotten Son is, then, absurd.

The logic used here is very similar to that used by the Arians. Arius, an ancient "heretic," argued that, since the Son was "begotten," he is not eternal. The Father must be "older" than the Son. He must have created a "Son" and then made the universe *through* his "begotten" Son. The Son is *like* the Father, Arius reasoned, in every respect except that he is "begotten" and, therefore, not eternal. Modern-day Jehovah's Witnesses continue the legacy of Arianism, the beliefs of those who followed Arius, by accepting his understanding of the nature of God and his Son.

At the fourth-century Council of Nicaea (325), the council fathers considered the matter of Arianism, an issue causing great division and confusion in the Church. Much of the debate centered on how to *express* the rival understandings represented at the council concerning the nature of the Son of God. Arius's followers agreed to use the Greek word, *homoiousios*, a term meaning *similar nature*, to express the relationship between the Father and Son. If we understand "nature" to mean *what* something is, the Arian position was that the Son is *similar* to the Father but, by the use of this term, it denied that the Son is *fully* God.

The trinitarian side rejected that term and, in its place, chose to express its position using another word: *homoousios*. The only spelling difference between the words is the lack of an *iota* (*i*). This apparently slight difference is actually indicative of a massive difference in meaning. *Homoousios* means "*same* nature." The Son, according to the trinitarians, is *fully* God and not merely similar to God.

The other term at the center of this controversy is the biblical term *begotten*. Bernard, like the Arians, defines this term as it is used with reference to human beings that are "born" in time. The Nicene fathers, however, focused on this term in contrast to another term that the Arians often used in its place: *made*. That the Son was begotten, the Arians argued, is identical to saying he was made or created.

These words are not synonyms, however. The product of one's creativity is not identical with a "begotten" child. I can "make," for instance, a work of art. I can "make" a book, a painting, a house, or a movie. I can also "beget" a child. The difference is apparent. The child proceeds from its parents as another instance of the *same kind of being* that they are. The things I make, on the other hand, express something about my nature but they are not the same kind of being I am. The Arian understanding of the term "begotten Son," confused this distinction. Arius's "Son of God" was of a different sort or category than the Father and therefore is more aptly described as a "made" Son rather than a begotten one.

It is important to note that the New Testament progressively unfolds the idea that Jesus' claims to divine sonship were claims to equality with God. Nowhere is this fact more clearly stated than in John 5:18. John comments that the desire of the authorities to kill Jesus grew because he "was calling God his own Father, making himself *equal* with God." This brief explanatory remark succinctly states the reasoning of the fourth-century trinitarians. Rather than arguing for the inferiority of the Son to the Father, the term *begotten* affirms in no uncertain terms the *equality* and *identity* of nature that exists between them. *What* the Father and Son are, then, is the same. The Nicene Creed expresses this conclusion when it states of the Son that he is *"begotten, not made*; one in *being (homoousios)* with the Father."

Consider my own sons. It is absurd to suggest that, because I am their father, they are less human than I. To *beget* a son is to produce *another* that is equal in nature to its parents. To a certain extent, then, when someone sees my children, they "see" me. This is an imperfect vision, of course, because of our various imperfections and differences that arise in the course of life experience. Since I am older than my children, for instance, I have more experiences and, hopefully, knowledge. If I could fully impart my nature in a *completely* perfect state to my children, they would be a perfect representation of my nature. This is not possible, of course, for two obvious reasons: (a) I am not perfect, and (b) we are born into this world in a state of potentiality toward the actualization of our nature. In other words, human nature, when we begin our life, is a framework or context for actualizing a host of possibilities. Exactly what in that massive range of possibilities will be actualized depends on the choices made and opportunities allowed to us. It is not possible for me to predict today what my children will make of themselves in the future. This is because, positively, they can be many things and, negatively, the limitations of our lifespan make it the case that they cannot actually become everything that is possible for them to be.

In any case, the New Testament uses the word "begotten" to modify the word *Son* in order to emphasize the sameness of nature that exists between the Son and his Father (John 1:18). I am not suggesting this is the only meaning of this word in the New Testament. Psalm 2:7, "You are my Son, this day have I begotten you," is a case in point. Psalm 2, a messianic psalm, likely uses these words to speak of the anointing of a special, chosen son of David to assume his throne. Certainly the New Testament applies these words to

Christ, the son of David *par excellence.* In Christ, the fullness of the meaning of God's Messiah as his "Son" is fulfilled. David was promised that he would have a son to whom God would be a "Father" (2 Sam. 7:12–14). These royal promises of a future king that would experience an unparalleled closeness to God are applied to Jesus in the New Testament (e.g., Heb. 1:5–6).

Bernard interprets the "day" of the Son's begetting, mentioned in Psalm 2:7, as the birth of Jesus in Bethlehem.[22] This reading is too facile, however. The New Testament applies this text, perhaps, to Jesus' birth but also to the Resurrection (Acts 13:33). The emphasis in New Testament interpretation, then, is not on a specific moment as much as on the whole earthly life of Jesus as the "moment" in history when the divine coronation takes place.

It is commonly recognized that the regal notion of "king" or messiah found in the Old Testament and in Jewish hopes around the time of Jesus was largely political and military in nature. The Messiah will come, it was believed, in order to destroy foreign occupation and set up a political kingdom in Jerusalem. When Jesus appeared speaking of the "kingdom of God" and working miracles, it was naturally assumed that he would make his way to Jerusalem, overcome the Romans, and, with the divine power he wielded, establish a universal kingdom. We can easily understand the disillusionment that followed Christ's "failure" upon arriving in Jerusalem. His betrayal by Judas and humiliating death at the hands of the Romans were simply incompatible with their messianic expectations.

The failure of prevailing modes of thought to explain the life, death, and resurrection of Jesus yielded a deeper penetration into the meaning of Christ's divine sonship. On the one hand, Jesus clearly did not fulfill the popular expectations of his time. On the other hand, his life cannot be ignored; if for no other reason than that there is good reason to believe he rose from the dead. Rather than being a failed, deluded "prophet," then, Jesus and his claims must be examined more carefully. His claims to "sonship," we discover, rather than having primary reference to an earthly king and kingdom, have a more *heavenly* meaning. Rather than understanding Jesus as a messiah who becomes God's son by his rise to regal power, he stands in relationship to God as *Son* from the first moments of his conscious life (Luke 2:49). In fact, as already discussed, we find that the Father and Son are in an eternal relationship of love. The messianic hopes of the Jews, then, for a messiah *made* God's Son are then surpassed by the revelation of God's Son in relationship to whom he has *always* been in communion.

For this reason, we may discern a dual significance to the expression "Son of God" and "begotten Son" within the New Testament. First, we have those texts that speak in reference to the Old Testament notion, and we have those that penetrate beyond that notion to a more spiritual, theological concept. Acts 13:33 likely expresses the first of these in its explanation of Psalm 2:7, while John 5:18 expresses the second. These observations are important not only for our purposes but also for a deeper appreciation of the development of Old Testament theology within the New Testament.

If the New Testament presents the words "only begotten Son" as bearing a deeper meaning than an earthly, messianic one, we must follow this meaning to its conclusion. Indeed, we must follow the meaning of these terms into the context of God's own nature, beyond the realm of history. As already discussed, the New Testament pushes us in this direction in various places that speak of the preexistence of Christ (John 1:1, 17:5, etc.).

Bernard argues that the terms "begotten" and "Son" "have *no meaning*" unless they speak of a "point in time" when that begetting takes place. We have already discovered that this is not true. These words carry the meanings of (a) sameness of nature and (b) distinction of persons, whether we introduce the notion of time or not. John 5:18 includes both of these meanings, but it is, by no means, the only meaningful text in this regard. When I speak of "my son," it is immediately clear that my son is (a) human and (b) not identical with me as a person.† When Jesus spoke of himself as God's Son, this was understood as a claim to be God (possessing the divine nature) and yet be distinct from the Father. Must we interpret these terms in a way that requires the temporal priority of the Father to the Son? In other words, is the Father "older" than the Son?

Oneness Pentecostals, in general, are conscious of the fact that the Bible, when it describes God, often uses *anthropomorphic* terminology. That is, the Bible makes frequent use of human bodily characteristics to describe God. Therefore we read of God's hands, eyes, ears, nose, feet, "backside," mouth, etc. Bernard explains, "The Bible describes infinite God in finite, human terms in order that we may better comprehend him."[23] We can agree that the human mind is incapable of fully understanding anything about God, who infinitely transcends our capacity to understand, and therefore we must use human experience and

---

† I am not suggesting that the term *God* is merely an abstract genus like *human*. Unlike humans and all other genera of creatures, there is only one instance of the divine substance. That substance is fully possessed by the three divine persons. It is not multiplied or distributed to many by way of matter. The point stands, however, that one "begotten" of another fully receives the nature of the begetter. In the case of creatures, the specific instances of a genus exist because of the external procession of offspring. Since God cannot be multiplied by external procession, the only distinctions within God are *internal*. See section below, "The *Best* Analogy."

speech to give us some measure of meaning, always admitting its imperfection.

A consequence of our human situation is that we must always qualify and define the sense(s) in which we are using terms. For instance, "right hand" is commonly a way of referring to divine power (e.g., Ps. 16:11). Since we use our hands, typically the right hand, to defend ourselves, it became a symbol of power. We hear by means of our ears, and therefore the "ear" became a symbol of listening or attentiveness (e.g., Ps. 88:2). If the Bible speaks of God's right hand or ears, then, we do not interpret these in crassly material and bodily senses but, instead, we find the primary intention of the terms and then discard all those things that are incompatible with the infinity and spirituality of God. Literal eardrums or bones and flesh are discarded. God's power and listening are real, however, although the perfection of God's power and listening far transcend our full comprehension. If we fail to make this distinction, the Bible will become hopelessly confusing. This is because there are various places where the Bible denies human imperfections of God (e.g., Num. 23:19). There are, of course, other places where God is likened to man by way of anthropomorphic speech.

Returning to the term "begotten Son," and the related issue of whether these words require temporality or the begetting of the Son in time, if we apply the principle of anthropomorphic language we discover that Bernard's conclusions are not only avoidable but also entirely unacceptable.

We have already located two meanings of "begotten Son" that should be incorporated into our understanding: (a) the Son is *one in nature* with the Father and (b) the Son is distinct from the Father. What remains is to consider what we must discard from the human usage of these terms in order to avoid contradiction with other known attributes of God. Two things immediately come to mind: time and change.

Time, at least in part, is the measurement of change. Change is the actualization of possibility. When we distinguish today from yesterday, we do so because the earth has turned in relationship to the sun as well as an incalculable number of other changes that have taken place. In fact, when we look carefully at this moment in contrast to a prior moment, we find a massive amount of flux that makes every moment different from any prior moment. Time, then, is the measurement of this flux or flow of change.

If we imagine a "timeless" being, we find one that does not *become* anything it was not before. We are all beings of time since we can speak about what we were, are, and shall be. A timeless being could not, in a technical sense, speak of what it "was," but simply that it "is." God, of course, is timeless inasmuch as he is not more perfect or complete today than he was "yesterday." For this reason, God stands apart from this flux of time in which we are immersed. With God, James wrote, "there is no shadow of turning" (James 1:17). Unlike the sun that casts its various shadows as it progresses across the sky, God casts no shadows resulting from change. The prophet Malachi makes the same point as he speaks God's words: "I, the Lord, do not change" (Mal. 3:10). We speak of God as "eternal" and "immutable." Of course, since we are so deeply immersed in both change and time, it is impossible for us to grasp God's way of being. In fact, when we try to comprehend these divine attributes, our minds either find them "boring" or static ways of being (since the loss of all time and change "stops" the flow of everything we know by experience), or devoid of meaning. We are forced to conceive of God's supreme manner of being through the limited grid of human terminology and experience. We've already seen that these facts mean our talk about God is always a humbling conversation, since we have to admit that God is ever greater than what our feeble language can express.

When we submerge the notion of "begotten Son" into the context of the eternal and infinite God, what "must be the case" in human experience ceases to hold true. Let us assume that the Father has a Son *within the framework of his eternity.* Suddenly we find that the Son "begotten" of the Father could never have begun to be Son. If God, within his eternity, *comes to have* a Son, then we have change and temporality within God, something we have already eliminated. While an eternally begotten Son in time is nonsensical (since time and eternity are fundamentally different), an eternally begotten Son in God's unchanging present is essential once one affirms a Son within the sphere of the divine nature.

There are other incompatible notions between God's eternity and our temporal existence in respect to our concept of "begetting." For instance, when I speak of my "son," implied is the presence of a mother. Also implied is a physical process of generation, including the sexual act and all the bodily, interior actions involved in procreation. Since "God is Spirit" (John 4:24), God's Son is not a physical offspring but an "exact imprint" or reflection of the Father (Heb. 1:3). God's spiritual nature requires that we conceive of the Son in spiritual terms. Jesus' remarks in a different context are relevant: "that which is born of the spirit *is spirit*" (John 3:6). In our present context, the physical elements of *begetting* fade away in favor of a spiritual act whereby the nature of the Father is *given to* the Son (and thereby "constituting" the Son) in an eternal act of love.

Further, the Son cannot be an *imperfect* representation of the Father, as is true in human experience. Instead, since

God does not change and is perfect, God's Son must always be the infinite realization or actualization of divine perfection. If God has a "Son," this Son is an unchangingly perfect expression of all that the Father is. What, then, is the *difference* between the Father and Son?

If the Son is the perfect and complete expression of the nature of the Father, the only difference between them would be, what theology calls, the "relationship of *origin*." In other words, the Son is begotten and the Father is not. As we already know, the Son's begetting is both spiritual and eternal. The designation of the Son as *begotten*, then, does not mean he began in time but that he originated in the eternal life of God *without beginning*. The notion of "origin" must be further examined. The Son's origin in the Father is not temporal (that is, restricted by time); that notion is excluded by God's eternity. The "origin" of the Son in the Father, then, is an eternal relationship whereby the Son proceeds from the Father. In that sense, then, we can speak of the Son's "dependence" on the Father. The Father "gives to" the Son all that he has, something Jesus frequently acknowledges. This eternal gift of the fullness of the Father's life to his Son, far from suggesting inferiority, affirms equality (e.g., John 5:26). We can no more envision a beginning to the Son than we can imagine the beginning of anything else that belongs to the essence of God.

It is a mistake to interpret this *internal* dependence of the Son on the Father as a mark of *substantial* inequality.[†] Even in human experience the temporal priority of a father to his son does not make the son less human than the father. Even though the father precedes the son, the son fully participates

---

† The Son is not a creation and therefore is not outside the divine nature. The Son is begotten by an *internal* procession so that the Son is not other than or outside of God.

in the meaning of being "human" and therefore is equal to the father in nature. There are, of course, various other inequalities in human experience, but these do not affect the point. We have already explained the source of those inequalities in the potentialities of our nature. Although "begotten" by the Father, then, the Son of God is a perfect, unchanging, and eternal expression of all the Father is. Consequently, we can speak of *sameness* and *equality* of nature, then, and yet difference in regard to the relationship of origin between the Father and Son.

One final word: The expression "begotten Son" is modified in John 1:18 by the Greek prefix "*mono*," meaning "only."† This qualifier indicates that there is no other Son like this one. Although the Bible speaks of Christians, for instance, as "children of God," it carefully qualifies this as a filial relationship resulting from *adoption* (Rom. 8:15), thereby indicating that we are not "begotten" by God in the full and proper sense of that term. We are "begotten" in a way that makes us true participants in God's salvation, but this is fundamentally different from the relationship between God and his Son. For this reason, Jesus never includes his address of God as *Father* with our own. To be sure, when he teaches us to pray he instructs us to say, "*our* Father." This is *our* instruction, however. His address of the Father is unique. This fact is unmistakable in all the Gospels. Matthew indicates the same point by his focus on the special mutual knowledge shared by Father and Son (11:27). Mark indicates it by the intimate words of Jesus in the garden: "*Abba*, Father" (14:36). Luke indicates it by his unique story of the boy Jesus who expresses surprise that his

---

† John 1:18, according to most scholars, should actually read, "the only begotten, *God*, who is in the bosom of the Father." If so, this verse is one of clearest statements of the divinity of the Son of God in a text that also emphasizes his relationship as "begotten" of the Father.

parents did not know "I had to be in *my Father's* house" (2:49).
John's Gospel is even clearer in its reference to Jesus' ascension
to "*my Father* and *your* Father" (20:17). Jesus carefully avoids
using "our" in this text and thereby maintains a vital distinction between himself and other "children of God."

Nowhere does Jesus or any New Testament writer claim
that our relationship to God is identical to that of Jesus. Jesus
is the unique Son of God. This, as we have seen, is because
he alone is *begotten* in the full sense of that word. Everything
the Father is has been imparted to the Son within the internal life of God himself. For this reason, he is fully God. Our
adoptive sonship allows us to share in Christ's relationship to
God, but this never makes us equal to him.

In conclusion, far from being meaningless, the *eternal*
generation of the Son of God is grounded in Scripture. It is
only nonsensical if we ignore the way the Bible speaks about
God. If we carefully search for the contextual meaning of
these terms and refuse to allow them meanings that cannot
apply to the eternal, immutable God, we will find they support the conclusions of the Nicene Council. The words of
the Creed are indeed meaningful: "We believe in one Lord
Jesus Christ, the only Son of God, *eternally begotten* of the
Father . . . *begotten not made, one in being* with the Father."

The Holy Spirit

Oneness Pentecostal theology often emphasizes the relative
lack of reference to the Holy Spirit, in contrast to Father and
Son both in the Bible and in literature on the subject of the
Trinity. For instance, I'm confident that in this chapter the
use of the terms *Father* and *Son* far exceeds any mention of
the Holy Spirit. Sometimes Oneness thinkers suggest this is
a problem for trinitarians. If God is truly a Trinity of divine
Persons, they ask, why does the Bible so frequently "ignore"

one of them? Additionally, the words "Holy Spirit" seem rather abstract or difficult to imagine.

The word "spirit," in both testaments, is one translation among several possible ones: spirit, breath, and wind. All these possible translations bring to mind invisible things. We discover their presence *indirectly*. I detect the presence of wind, for instance, by limbs or leaves that move under its influence or by its press against my skin. I know someone is breathing because of the movement of his chest or sounds coming from him. It is difficult to speak directly about "spirit" without making some reference to its activities or effects. Indeed, Oneness Pentecostals most frequently speak of the Holy Spirit as an experience, typically the experience of speaking in tongues.

It is relatively easy to produce a concrete mental image or concept when we use the terms *father* and *son*. Our own life experience is probably sufficient. Of course, these concepts may hinder our ability to understand what those terms mean when used in reference to God, but they at least provide a starting point. The Holy Spirit, however, is more difficult, since we have no mental "picture" of a spirit with the exception of effects produced by "spirit." Yves Congar, for example, in his introductory words to his massive work on this subject, speaks of a "certain lack of conceptual mediation."[24]

It is nonetheless true, however, that the Bible speaks of the Holy Spirit and identifies the Spirit with God. Indeed, there are texts in which the terms *God* and *Holy Spirit* are used interchangeably (Acts 5:3–5; 1 Cor. 3:16; 6:19). Of course, the Bible speaks of God as both holy and a spirit and therefore the combination of these terms causes no immediate confusion. Difficulty enters, however, when we try to explain what exactly the Bible means by it.

Bernard is certainly correct when he explains that *Holy Spirit* "emphasizes a particular aspect of God."[25] He goes on to explain that it refers to God's work "among all men everywhere" and his desire to "fill and indwell human lives."[26] In Luke's writings, the New Testament texts that most frequently use this expression, the Holy Spirit is typically mentioned alongside some dynamic, powerful act of God of historical significance. Acts 2:4 and 4:31, for instance, mention the Holy Spirit "filling" the disciples. In the first case, the disciples are enabled to speak languages they had never learned. In the second case, they receive extraordinary boldness to proclaim the gospel of Christ. References to the Holy Spirit alongside such important "signs" of God's presence are the rule in Luke's writings rather than the exception. It is reasonable to conclude, then, that the Bible often refers to the Holy Spirit in order to emphasize God's active presence in a particular historical moment. The active presence of God is known by the evidences or signs produced by God's Spirit.

The term *spirit*, and all its alternate translations, suggests power, presence, and action. It is a dynamic term. It is often used in schools to speak of enthusiasm and excitement that bind the students together ("school spirit"). If "spirit" or "breath" is lacking, there is no life. God's Holy Spirit certainly speaks of God's active, dynamic, and living presence. Paul's writings testify to this conclusion by their many references to "fruit" and "gifts" of the Spirit, all of which emphasize the results *produced by* the Spirit's presence (1 Cor. 12, Gal. 5:22-23). Paul also speaks of the newness brought by Christ as "*life* in the Spirit" (Rom. 8:9ff). Over and again we find dynamic evidences of God's presence when we see references to God's Spirit.

If this were the extent of the biblical data, we would be content to conclude that the Holy Spirit is simply a way of referring to God's presence and action in history. Perhaps we could describe the same point another way: the Holy Spirit is God proceeding into human history in order to produce recognizable signs of his life and love. Arguably the most striking Pauline text expressing this meaning is Romans 5:5: "The love of God has been poured out within our hearts through the Holy Spirit who was given to us." In light of the New Testament message, it is not overreaching to suggest that the Holy Spirit extends God's love to the human family. God's love is understood both objectively and subjectively. We discover that God loves us by the Spirit's work, and we also experience love at work *in us* by the same Spirit.

All the biblical data cannot be explained by this simple definition, however. The definition we have discovered is certainly true and important, but it awaits further development.

First, we must remind ourselves of Matthew 28:19. Here the Holy Spirit is distinguished from the Father and Son. We have already discovered that the Father and Son are one in nature but distinct as persons. It is reasonable to suppose that the same should be extended to the Holy Spirit; otherwise, the list is hard to explain. If the Holy Spirit is God, something we have already accepted, it is reasonable to conclude that he is distinct from the Father and Son, since this is true of the first two terms in Matthew 28:19.

Second, the Bible uses similar language of the Holy Spirit that we found in reference to the relationship between Father and Son. John 14–16 is the most important section in Scripture in regard to establishing this claim; although, of course, it is not the only relevant text. Jesus spoke at length of the coming of the Holy Spirit who, he says, would be *sent* by the Father (John 14:26). He further indicates that the Holy Spirit will "teach" the disciples and "remind" them of Jesus' teachings. Later he will speak of the "procession" of the Holy Spirit

from the Father (John 15:26). It is easy to show that many
of these terms are associated with Jesus' relationship to the
Father ("sent," "proceeds"). Jesus' words leave no room for
doubt, however. The Holy Spirit is *not* identical with the Son.
Jesus includes himself with the Father in sending the Spirit
(John 15:26). Jesus also says the Spirit will "bear witness" of
the Son. If this is not clear enough, Jesus later describes the
future work of the Spirit and states, "He will not speak on his
own initiative, but whatever he hears, he will speak . . . he
shall glorify me; for he shall take of mine, and shall disclose
it to you" (John 16:13–15). The interaction between Father,
Son, and Holy Spirit is unmistakable. The Father "sends"
both the Son and Spirit. The Spirit is "sent" by the Father and
Son. The Holy Spirit "hears" from the Father, testifies of the
Son, does not speak on his own initiative, etc. This language,
if we take it seriously, forces us to think of the Father, Son,
and Holy Spirit as personally distinct from each other.

Bernard addresses these texts in John's Gospel by placing
strong emphasis on 14:17–18.[27] Jesus assures his disciples that
the Spirit is now "with" them and will be "in" them. This
is taken to mean that Jesus' presence with them was nothing else than the Holy Spirit. Jesus would leave in bodily
form but would return in a spiritual form to dwell in them.
Even though the chapter speaks of the Holy Spirit in a way
that might lead us to think of him as distinct from the Son,
he is actually identical with the Son, a fact Jesus makes apparent here. If one is inclined to doubt this interpretation,
Bernard directs attention to verse 18: "I will not leave you
as orphans; *I will come to you.*" What could be clearer? Jesus is
identifying himself with the coming Holy Spirit.

In reference to the many texts cited above about the Spirit,
one may justly wonder why the Gospel would use such apparently misleading language in order to make a simple point;

if, of course, Bernard's interpretation is correct. The Oneness interpretation, however, is not compelling. John 14:18 is clearly a reference to the post-Resurrection appearances of Jesus. Verse nineteen is an explanation of that verse and is clearly a prediction of the Resurrection: "After a little while the world will behold me no more; but you will behold me; because I live, you shall live also." The brief absence of Jesus followed by his appearances to his apparently abandoned disciples will convince them that through Christ true life, culminating in their own resurrection, can be possessed. In reference to verse seventeen, there is no reason we should not take this as a reference to the presence of the Holy Spirit in connection with Christ's ministry; a fact emphasized in all the Gospels (e.g., John 1:33), beginning most distinctly with his baptism by John. The power of God's Spirit in relationship to the ministry of Christ would extend to the ministry and life of the early Christian Church. None of this, however, requires that we identify the person of the Son with that of the Spirit. We may speak of a close relationship between them, but that much is evident in the language of the texts already cited in John 14–16.

Bernard explains the meaning of Jesus' references to "sending" the Holy Spirit. "Jesus went to heaven in His glorified body so he could form a new relationship with His disciples, by sending back his own Spirit as the Comforter."[28] In light of the fact, however, that Jesus indicates the Holy Spirit would not "speak on his own initiative," etc., are we really to think that the *humanity* of Jesus sent the divine Spirit into the world? Is this an instance of the human nature *directing* the divine nature? Bernard's explanations avoid this conclusion. The alternative, however, is to admit that Jesus is speaking of sending the Spirit from his divine consciousness. The Son of God, along with the Father, will send the

Holy Spirit. This conclusion is far too close to trinitarianism to bring comfort to Oneness thinkers.

Does all this talk of the Holy Spirit suggest the *subordination* or inferiority of the Holy Spirit to the Father and Son? The answer is "no" if we understand the biblical language about the Holy Spirit similarly to the way we understood the language about the Son. The Holy Spirit "proceeds" from the Father and is "sent" by the Father and Son. Both these terms are used of the Son. Jesus also frequently speaks of his full determination to do the will of his Father; a will that he delights in fulfilling. The Holy Spirit, too, delights in doing the will of the Father. Although mysteriously veiled behind his work of illuminating the meaning of Christ, the Holy Spirit is clearly distinguished from the Father and Son and yet placed in the same divine "sphere" (Matt. 28:19).

Why is the Holy Spirit not mentioned as frequently as the Father and Son? Perhaps the explanation is found in the inspiration of Holy Scripture. If the Bible is truly inspired by God's Spirit (2 Pet. 1:21), and the mission of the Spirit is to illuminate the human mind in respect to the truth of Christ, the Son, the relative lack of reference to the Holy Spirit is exactly what we would expect.

Years ago I heard someone liken this fact to a photographer.[†] We have many pictures in our home that we have taken through the years. My image, however, is relatively rare. This is because I am typically the one taking the pictures. The "illusion" is that I am absent when, in fact, I am present, by implication, in each of them. My presence is found precisely in the reality of the pictures. Scripture is

---

† My recollection is that I first heard this illustration used by Evangelical theologian Robert Bowman in a public debate on the Trinity with Robert Sabin, a Oneness Pentecostal.

the product of the Holy Spirit, and it tells us the story he wishes to reveal. To be sure, there are many references to the Holy Spirit, but their mystery and deference to the Son are striking and reinforce Christ's words: "he shall speak of me."

What is the *difference* between the Holy Spirit and the Father and Son? With reference to the Father we may easily answer: the Son is begotten and the Holy Spirit proceeds from him, but the Father is not begotten and does not proceed. With reference to the Son, we may answer: he proceeds from the Father by generation, or, in other words, he is begotten of the Father. We may also note that he sends the Holy Spirit along with the Father.† What about the Holy Spirit, though? Negatively we can say that the Holy Spirit is not the Father or the Son. The Holy Spirit does not "beget" the Son nor is the Spirit begotten. He proceeds from the Father in a different way from the Son. Perhaps the key to answering this question is found in the word *spirit*. This term suggests dynamic movement and love. Love and desire are associated most closely with the will. Since both the Father and Son send the Spirit, we may tentatively conclude that the Spirit is the personal procession of love from both Father and Son. Since "love" is less tangible than a "begotten Son," it is understandable that we have trouble expressing the precise meaning of the Spirit in contrast to Father and Son. Love, by its very nature, directs us to lovers: in this case, Father and Son. The Holy Spirit, then, is the unique procession of love from the Father and

† I avoid raising the *filioque* controversy. Suffice it to say, however, the Bible does not explicitly state that the Holy Spirit proceeds from the Son. Theologically, however, we must note (a) if the only difference between the Father and Son is that the Son is begotten and the Father is not and (b) the Son fully expresses the essence of the Father, it follows that the Spirit proceeds from the Son as from the Father. It should also be noted that the Bible speaks of the Spirit as "of the Father" and "of the Son" (e.g., Gal. 4:6).

132 ALL IN THE NAME

Son. This procession is not abstract or impersonal but, rather, supremely personal.[†]

Does the Trinity Make Sense?

One of the things about Jesus that made him a great teacher is the fact that he was able to capture the imagination of his audiences by using stories. These stories, we call them *parables*, illustrate spiritual truths by means of images drawn from the everyday lives of one's listeners. The word *parable* itself is derived from a Greek word that literally means "to lay alongside." Jesus placed scenes from earthly, physical existence next to spiritual truths. The earthly experiences of human beings and of nature provide "windows" into the spiritual world.

As we seek to understand the nature of God, to the degree that we are able to do so, we struggle to find illustrations that will help us "imagine" what God is like. The biblical writers do a good deal of this as they liken God to a "rock," bringing to mind the notions of stability and trustworthiness; or a bird that cares for and protects its young; or a "consuming fire" that eliminates impurities and serves as a sign of judgment. The Bible is filled with such analogies and illustrations. They help stimulate the imagination and enable us to *see*, albeit imperfectly, what God is like.

Oneness Pentecostals, as noted, try to develop their own analogies and comparisons to illustrate what God is like. They are fond of using the plurality of relationships that individual persons can have to others. A man can be a father, son, and husband at the same time and yet be a single person. This illustration quickly clarifies the meaning of "three modes" or "roles," terms often used when describing the Oneness notion

---

† For a thorough discussion of the biblical and theological issues pertaining to the Holy Spirit, see Yves Congar, *I Believe in the Holy Spirit* (3 vols.).

of God. The three forms water can take (liquid, solid, gas) are often used to make the same point. Sometimes trinitarians unwittingly make use of the same analogy. The Trinity, however, is not the claim that God "becomes" Father and then Son and then Holy Spirit, depending on the external conditions in which God is "placed." The Trinity professes that Father, Son, and Holy Spirit are, though one in being, simultaneously and eternally in relationship toward each other.

Through the centuries, trinitarians have sought helpful illustrations that shed some light on exactly what is meant when we speak of the Trinity. I remember reading a children's book on this subject many years ago. The book's cover featured an apple with a slice from its side. The peel, "meat," and core of the apple were visible. The book likened the three "parts" of the apple to the three divine Persons of the Trinity. Although the apple is a *single* apple it is nonetheless divisible into three *parts*. Numerous other analogies drawn from the physical world have been used (e.g., three-leaf clovers; the sun's light, heat, and rays).

Although such illustrations can be helpful, especially when used with children, they disclose fundamental inadequacies when seriously examined. There are two apparent problems with illustrations for the Trinity drawn from the visible, physical world. First, most of them are not based on interpersonal relationships but on impersonal things. Second, they illustrate how "parts" of things can be united into a single organism or entity. Trinitarian theology, however, refuses to use "parts" in its vocabulary. The Father is not "part" of God. The divine Persons of the Trinity are not like three pieces of a pie that, when considered on their own, are "one-third" of God, but, when combined together, are "all" of God. The nature of God is not divisible into "parts" that are somehow united together like the pieces of a puzzle or the parts of a model airplane.

Of course, we cannot ask too much of analogies. They are typically helpful in making a single observation. The various analogies drawn from the world of nature are by no means perfect, but they can nudge the mind toward understanding by their focus on things that are both plural and singular.

The Best Analogy

The best of the Catholic tradition, however, has not focused on these kinds of analogies. St. Augustine, for example, was convinced that some "vestiges" of the Trinity exist in the creation.[†] If God is a Trinity of divine Persons, it should be possible to find some helpful analogy in God's world. Since the Trinity is the highest of all realities, it is reasonable that we shall find the best analogy in the highest kinds of existence in the creation. Consequently, the best analogy for the Trinity will be found through reflection on men and angels, not on apples and rocks. There is something about human persons (and angels) that makes us more like God. Since we lack direct knowledge of the angelic way of being, we will have to settle for human existence as our primary analogy.

Genesis 1:26 sets the creation of the human family on the sixth creative day apart from the creation of all lower life on the prior days. What sets the man apart is that he was created "in the *image* of God." Contextually, the apparent meaning of this line is that man was given "dominion" over the natural world. On a deeper level, however, we may

---

† See St. Augustine, *On the Trinity* IX–XV. Augustine develops several different analogies in his work. The analogy developed here is most similar to his presentation in book IX. I owe whatever value this analogy may have to readers to insights gleaned from Augustine and Aquinas. I once thought analogies based on the mind are inadequate since, in focusing on *one* mind, I thought they supported a conclusion more similar to modalism than trinitarianism. My reading of St. Thomas Aquinas convinced me otherwise. Since discovering its value, I have used it in the classroom and find students most often consider it intriguing and compelling.

justly ask what it is that allows man to have this dominion. The answers traditionally given are two: (a) intellect and (b) freedom. The *intellect* allows us to rise above our environment and concerns for immediate survival, pleasure, and pain. Even though our physical strength, sense powers, and reflexes are often inferior to other animals, we populate zoos with them, but there are no zoos operated by animals in which humans are on exhibit. We are able to understand the *nature* of the world, including its animal inhabitants, and thereby exercise dominion over it. As a result, humans can learn to grow crops, build skyscrapers and musical instruments, develop various math and science disciplines, write books about these disciplines, and worship God. All of these require abstraction and transcendence above one's environment. From all appearances, the other animals are incapable of producing these effects. Researchers spend years with primates and dolphins trying to demonstrate they are capable of these activities. The results are often interesting, but paltry when compared with the capabilities of a five-year-old child.

Freedom of the will is the second unique feature of the human person. Only the human person, not the rest of the animal world, was forbidden to eat of the tree of the knowledge of good and evil at the center of the Garden of Eden. This image of the "tree" speaks of the primordial (and perennial) temptation to be our own "god": to determine what good and evil will be *on our own*, apart from the declared will of God. This scene may be the most embarrassing and destructive of our history; however, it also speaks of the greatness of the human person. We are able to direct our own path toward happiness. We can choose to discover true life in relationship to God. By the same token, however, we may choose not to direct our lives toward God and, as a result, bring misery upon ourselves.[†] The fact that we place humans on trial for their actions and hold them morally responsible, but do not hold lower animals similarly responsible, speaks of our implicit awareness of the unique human gift of freedom.

Although the "image of God" may mean more than what we have described here, it certainly does not mean less. It is our intellect and will that set us apart from the rest of the world around us. It is here, Augustine and Aquinas argue, we shall find the highest analogy for the Trinity.

The Inward Turn

Let us examine our minds by turning *inward*. We discover, by this inward turn, that our mind is a mysterious realm, very different from the outside world. Many of the things we take for granted about the material world no longer apply in the case of the mind. It makes sense to ask, for instance, how heavy or how tall the books are sitting next to me. It makes no sense to ask how heavy or how tall my thoughts are, however.

Not only are my thoughts of a different sort than objects I observe outside myself, but they also populate an interior "world" that is unique to me. No one else can enter the world of my mind; unless, of course, by means of language I share with them what I am thinking. My mind belongs to

† The traditional Catholic understanding of the human person includes the notion that the root cause of our longings for happiness and truth is a longing for the absolute Good and True: God. Even if a person lacks a clear, conscious awareness of God as the "end" or goal of our longings, God is still their ultimate aim. Consequently, we are never finally and completely happy through obtaining finite, limited "goods." The human situation is then inherently frustrating since the powers of our soul are only brought to true rest in the presence of a reality that transcends the world of created beings. "Sin" for persons without explicit knowledge of God is their failure to be faithful to the impulse to goodness and truth—something that happens in countless ways, especially by treating a finite "good" as absolute goodness. For instance, a person considers making money or sensual pleasure the supreme goal of their life.

me and is the context in which reflection and choices are made. What I say and do, in a distinctly human way, originates in my mind. I am now choosing to write these words. This choice started in my mind as a book on this subject was envisioned.

In these few short words we have seen, by reflection, that our mind is the "home" or realm in which thoughts are contemplated and choices are made. Each of these powers, the power of thought and the power of will, belong to the mind. *Together* they constitute our interior life.

The Mind's Unity

There is another interesting feature of these aspects of the mind that should be noted. *My thoughts and will are not separable from my mind.* In other words, I cannot take my thoughts *as such* and give them separate existence. I can, of course, try to communicate my thoughts to others. In fact, I am doing that now. The words on this page comprise a collection of "signs," signs that point to realities that are present in my mind now. My hope is that you will decipher these signs and come to think the thoughts that are now present in me. By communicating these thoughts by means of the signs of written language, I do not lose my own thoughts. In giving them to you, I still possess them. My thoughts proceed within my mind, but they do so in such a way that they remain within me. It makes no sense to speak of my thoughts as something *separate* or separable from me. The same is true of my acts of will. My choices may result in effects outside me, but those choices ever remain my own. Those choices shape my character and tend to form habits, good or bad, that reside in my will.

The interior processions of thought and willful acts differ significantly from exterior acts of procession. Consider the conception and birth of a child. The child "proceeds" from its parents. It truly comes from the parents. Similarly, my thoughts and will come from my mind. They are different, however, in that the child is now a separate being from the parents. The parents will likely pass away before the child's life concludes. The death of the parents does not entail the death of the child. My thoughts and will, however, although they "proceed" from my mind, *exist only in union with my mind*. If my mind were to die, my thoughts and will would die with it. I mean, of course, my thoughts and will inasmuch as they are present to *my* mind. My current conscious life, including its thoughts and choices, is a *whole* that survives together or dies together.

Let me restate the analogy and take it a step further. I am thinking about the subject of this chapter. These thoughts belong to me and reside in me. I am "sending them forth" in the form of words. This sending, however, does not mean they have left my mind. My thoughts are proceeding in two distinct ways: interiorly and exteriorly. My thoughts proceed *within* me and *outside* me. The difference between the two is that the interior processions remain an aspect of me whereas the exterior procession becomes something other than me, although related to me. If I cease to exist, these words may remain on pieces of paper while the thoughts, as existing within me, no longer exist.

Implicit in what has already been said, it is apparent that the interior life of the mind contains three basic distinctions. First, there is the *mind* itself that is the "home" or context for reflection. Second, there are the objects that the mind contemplates (*thought*). Third, there are the choices we make with regard to what we contemplate (*will*). All mental activity can be placed into one of these three categories: mind, thought, and will.

It should be noted that it is the mind that, equipped with the faculties described above, allows us to contemplate and "know" God. This is because God is spirit (John 4:24). The call to union with God is not a physical union but a union of thought and will. We are called to know and love God. Both are acts of the mind. We may also speak of the mind as the center of our spiritual life since, as we have already considered, the mind's contents have very different "objects" than do the bodily senses.

There is, then, a threefold distinction within the human mind. These distinctions are real but inseparable and, therefore, together constitute our single mental awareness or conscious life. We may be aware of interior conflict between, for instance, what we *know* and what we *will*. This conflict is not between alien entities, however; both reside within and are aspects of our single mental life, however much it may be conflicted within.

God: The Supreme Mind

Imagine a *supreme spiritual being*, fully equipped with mind, thought, and will. If we were to contrast this mind with our own, there would be fundamental differences. First, it would have no lack in understanding. Second, there would be no conflict between the different aspects of this mind. Third, there would be no passions or desires for things that are ultimately not for its good. In other words, its thoughts and will would be harmonious and complete. Additionally, if it is truly perfect, it is self-sufficient, since it would need nothing other than itself for its perfection.

Let us continue our thought experiment by imagining this supreme mind as *infinite*. If this mind is infinite and perfect, its primary *object* of contemplation would also share in these attributes. In other words, the *thought* of this supreme mind would be infinitely perfect, too, and therefore a *perfect* mirror image or reflection of that mind. In fact, we may speak of this infinite thought as a *self-thought*. If the divine self-thought possesses infinity and perfection, it will be identical to the mind from which it proceeds, with the one exception that it proceeds or comes from the mind while the mind produces or causes its self-thought.[†]

Think of your own self. This thought is a very inadequate expression of you. First, there are many things about you that your self-thought simply excludes. Perhaps this is simply because you have forgotten them or would prefer not to think about them. Further, because of the imperfection of our minds, it is simply not possible to hold together everything about anything we think about all at once. A supremely perfect mind would, in thinking about itself, exhaustively and perfectly "mirror" itself in such a thought. Infinite self-thought is proper to such a mind since, as infinite, it finds supreme delight in contemplating infinite perfection.

We have not considered the will that also proceeds from this infinite mind. Will, as already discussed, is interior, mental *desire*.[‡] We want, for instance, to be happy. The desire for happiness is the proper object of the will. Just as our bodily senses have "proper" objects, so does the will. Our eyes, for example, are oriented toward grasping light and shapes. Our eyes do not hear, however. Our ears do not see. This is because these senses are oriented toward particular objects. In order to determine what the function of a particular power is,

---

† I am not suggesting a perfect mind cannot contemplate imperfect objects (like us!). I would follow Aquinas on this point who reasoned that God sees all his *effects* in seeing himself perfectly (*Summa Theologiae* I.14.5).

‡ I am excluding consideration here of the bodily passions that exercise an influence on our choices. Since these are shared common with lower creatures, they are not, strictly speaking, essential or helpful for the analogy.

then, we have to identify its proper object or intended goal. The intellect's proper object is *truth*. We want to know truth by means of the intellect. We don't want to know lies; we want to know truth. The will moves toward what is perceived as *good*. We deem something good if we find it desirable. Even if something is not truly good for us, we only choose to obtain it if we somehow perceived it or convince ourselves that it is truly good for us. The end result of our desire to obtain truth and goodness is interior contentment or happiness. The *will* is that interior longing for goodness that contributes (hopefully) to our actually achieving a measure of the happiness that motivates our desire to act.

From these observations we may observe that the will presupposes both the mind and thought. If we don't know about something, we can't have a desire for it. We would only read a book, for instance, if we had some reason to think it may be interesting or advantageous to us. If we discover that we were wrong about that "thought," we will put the book aside. The will can act upon only what it has some knowledge of, even if that knowledge turns out to be misguided.

If there is a supreme, infinitely perfect mind, possessing mind, thought, and will, the will would follow upon and, therefore, on some level, *depend on* mind and thought. This is because the will flows from the mind as its point of origin, but also follows thought since it cannot desire what it does not know. The supreme mind's will would, then, flow or proceed from both mind and thought.

Additionally, the infinitely perfect "will" that exists in this supreme mind would, as infinitely perfect, be indistinguishable from mind and thought except insofar as it proceeds from them both. In other words, the supreme will is not a partial expression of the supreme mind but fully possesses its infinite perfections, while also standing in a relationship toward the other two aspects of that supreme mind that allows it to be distinguished from them but, by no means, separated.

Mind, Thought, and Will: Father, Son, and Holy Spirit

If the reader has followed this analogy, its application should be taking shape. Within the nature of God, we have discovered, there are three distinctions: Father, Son, and Holy Spirit. The Son and Holy Spirit proceed from the Father by a spiritual procession. The Son is strikingly similar to the features we discovered about "thought" in the infinite mind just described. "Thought" *depends on* mind but perfectly mirrors it. Similarly, the Son perfectly mirrors the Father but is distinct from him. It is also worthy of note that Scripture speaks of the Son as the *Logos*, or "thought" that is eternally with God, the Father (compare John 1:1 and 1 John 1:2).

Further, the Holy Spirit, as already discussed, is depicted as the "love" of God proceeding outward. Love, of course, is the positive movement of one's will toward another. The word *spirit* itself suggests dynamic movement and desire. We also find that the Spirit is "sent" by both the Father and Son, suggesting the proper order of the divine "persons" is Father, Son, and *then* Spirit. This is consistent with the analogy in which will logically follows both mind and thought.

The human mind, then, provides a fruitful analogy for the Trinity. There are obvious differences, of course. They are too numerous to mention. Perhaps the most obvious difference is the finitude of our minds in contrast to God's. This means that our thoughts, for instance, will not be an infinitely perfect "image" of ourselves, but will always be a partial expression of who we are. The second obvious difference is that we are single persons, whereas within God's essence are three Persons. The three distinctions within us that *partially* express our nature, when magnified to infinity, become three infinitely perfect divine Persons that are inseparably one in the divine unity.

Although the analogy limps in some ways (what else can we expect?), it is also powerfully revealing. It provides an analogy for God's unity in that, although it is possible to *distinguish* the mind's aspects, it is not possible to *separate* them. It provides an analogy for inseparable *threeness* within God by recognizing the threeness that exists within the oneness of our minds. It provides an analogy based on a spiritual reality (i.e., the mind). This immediately gives it an advantage over analogies based on the material world. The analogy is also valuable in that it directs us to the proper context for understanding what key terms mean in the expression of the Trinity (e.g., procession, *Logos*, Father, Son, Holy Spirit).

The analogy also has the advantage of showing a *correspondence* between God's creation and God's revelation. Although we certainly cannot conclude from this analogy that we have *proven* the Trinity through reason alone, we have, enlightened by divine revelation in Christ and Scripture, discovered an echo and "vestige" of the Trinity within the human person, made in God's image.

Of What Practical Value Is the Trinity?

"I've never heard a preacher get excited about the Trinity!" I've heard this claim a number of times through the years. It was often argued that the Trinity was not only illogical, but it is simply a dry, dull belief.

I'd like to conclude this chapter by reflecting on this claim. I do not doubt that my pastor was speaking the truth based on his experience. He likely never heard a trinitarian preacher or teacher address the subject of the Trinity in anything other than an academic disposition. I firmly believe, however, that the Trinity is the most profound and enriching of all Christian beliefs. The *Catechism of the Catholic Church* states,

> The mystery of the Most Holy Trinity is *the central mystery of Christian faith and life*. It is the mystery of God in himself. It is therefore the source of all the mysteries of faith, the light that enlightens them. It is the most fundamental and essential teaching in the "hierarchy of the truths of faith."[29]

A "mystery," in common theological usage, is a truth revealed by God that is not fully comprehensible by the human mind. It is important to note that this does not mean that a mystery is a contradiction or illogical. To the contrary, a mystery ever invites our contemplation. Contradictions do not invite contemplation since they are without real meaning. There are, of course, meaningful paradoxes. Indeed, we often find the most fruitful insights of our experience in "solving" paradoxes. Earlier, for instance, we mentioned the idea that individual humans discover meaning and happiness within social life or community. This fact is paradoxical inasmuch as it brings individuality into relationship with the community. That the two are inseparably intertwined may seem initially paradoxical, but, upon reflection, they are found to complement each other quite nicely.

Another good example, this one more specifically theological, is the "two natures of Christ" discussed above. Sometimes we find Jesus acting in such a way that we conclude he was truly a man; at other times he speaks and acts in ways that suggest he is far more than a man. These two truths are, perhaps, paradoxical, but not contradictory. We may, to some degree, relieve the tension between these two affirmations as we reflect on what Scripture reveals about the identity of Jesus.

Although a mystery is not a contradiction, we cannot claim to ever fully penetrate its meaning. A mystery ever beckons further reflection and growing insight. This growth in insight is *never complete*. A mystery ever eludes our full comprehension. A mystery invites a response like that of the apostle Paul in his contemplation on God's sovereignty and purposes in this world: "Oh, the depth of the riches both of the wisdom and knowledge of God! How unsearchable are his judgments and unfathomable his ways! For who has known the mind of the Lord, or who became his counselor? . . . For from him and through him and to him are all things. To him be the glory forever. Amen" (Rom. 11:33–36).

Our *thinking* about God, then, should ultimately yield to *doxology*, or worship. The human mind, if it is thinking clearly, is always conscious of the infinite depths of the divine mystery that far exceed our abilities. St. Thomas liked to quote Aristotle's words, "Our knowledge of God is like the light of the sun to the eye of the owl." The light of the sun overpowers our eyes and forces them to look away. In a much greater way, the direct vision of God is beyond our powers. Theology, then, leads to humility and worship. This is what we mean by mystery. To the extent that theology fails to produce this effect, it has failed.

Theoretical and Practical Knowledge

The Trinity, the *Catechism* informs us, is *the central mystery* of Christian faith. This statement is necessarily true. If God is eternally a Trinity of divine Persons, it follows that everything else that God does or reveals flows from God's triune life. Our theology should reflect this central place of the

Trinity, and also relate every other affirmation of faith to this supreme "fount" of all reality. If everything that God has done in history is an expression of his triune life, we can relate back to the Trinity the various truths that become known throughout the history of divine revelation.

This fact is most evident when we arrive at the pinnacle of divine revelation: Jesus Christ. It is commonly agreed that we discover the mystery of the Trinity in and through the words, life, and death of Jesus. This, again, is quite reasonable since Christ is the incarnate "Word" of the Father, proceeding forth from the interior life of God. If God were to tell us about the highest and deepest truth of all reality, it stands to reason that he would express this concurrently with the supreme moment of revelation.

Further, we should not think of the Trinity only in terms of practical value. Some truths are worth contemplating for their own sake. This is part of the uniqueness and nobility of human persons. We can gain deep joy and happiness by contemplating truth, not just by gaining some "practical" effect. The distinction between practical and theoretical sciences serves as an example. A practical science is one engaged for the sake of some practical "end" or benefit. The study of medicine, for instance, has as its goal the health of the body. The study of architecture has the goal of building aesthetically pleasing, durable, safe structures.

There are other sciences, however, that are not initially motivated by a practical application. I suspect that Copernicus theorized about the orbit of the earth in relationship to the sun for the sake of knowing the truth of the matter. He certainly did not engage this question because it would help him grow crops more effectively. A theoretical science is studied in order to enrich one's understanding, not primarily to gain some other effect.

The study of God should be primarily motivated by the desire to know God as he is in himself and in his revelation. The interior fulfillment that results is sufficient benefit. I often explain to my students that my choice to study theology was not motivated by the desire to make money. I did not, as a high school graduate, look over my options and select theology because I thought it would yield the largest payday or be the least difficult task. To the contrary, I gave no thought to any of these matters. My chief concern was to *know*, to understand, the truths revealed by God.

Some years ago, while doing graduate work in philosophy, one of my beloved professors invited us students to stay after our classes to translate some Latin texts of the Muslim philosopher, Avicenna. Since we had to learn to translate Latin texts, we accepted the invitation. I recall struggling to translate a particular text that had to do with the reasons why Avicenna rejected an infinite regress of finite causes and, therefore, concluded that an infinite, self-existent cause of every finite thing must exist. My professor asked me to explain the meaning of this argument. I confidently explained what I thought was the sense of the argument. He tersely remarked that I did not understand the point. I asked him to explain my error. He told me to go and study the matter. I did. I came back and explained the subject again; he again informed me that I was missing the point. I continued to study. In fact, one night I had a dream about this philosophical problem! I told my professor about this dream, and he, with a smile, said, "Then you may be fit for a career in philosophy. What you find yourself dreaming about at night is probably what you love most."

Our contemplation of God should be motivated by a desire to know the God who made us and saved us, not because we can use it for some practical benefit. The contemplation of

God himself is the supremely worthy goal of human thought, and therefore is sufficient justification in itself.

That being said, however, it should be possible to show the connection between the highest truths about God and what God has done in history, including what is revealed about the practical Christian life. This connection between what God is and how he is revealed in the context of human history is vital to understanding the unity of God's purposes.[†] If we are correct, "excitement" or enthusiasm about any aspect of Christian faith should give rise to corresponding enthusiasm and excitement about the Trinity, the root cause of all the other related truths.

The Passion of Christ

It is difficult to argue with the observation that the central focus of the biblical story is Jesus Christ. Christians understand the Old Testament as an extended period of preparation for the eventual appearance of Christ, the incarnate Son of God. The New Testament explains the meaning of Christ by way of historical summaries of his public life, death, and resurrection (Gospels) and by way of various books applying and explaining the message of Christ to his followers (Letters).

The "meaning" of Christ is not presented, however, by way of an exhaustive biographical treatment. To the contrary, it is often noted that the Gospels are not biographies in the modern sense. They focus on a relatively short period

---

†   Classically this distinction is made by speaking of God *in himself* as the *ontological* Trinity and God *as revealed in human history* as the *economic* Trinity. We discover the economic Trinity first, since we are creatures of time and history. We discover the immanent Trinity by inference to the eternal life of God from God's actions as known in time. Trinitarian theology insists on a real connection between the two. We truly discover what God is like in himself by reflection on his actions in time.

of time in the life of Jesus. They say almost nothing of his childhood and young adult life. Their focus is almost exclusively on Christ's public ministry, a ministry inaugurated by his baptism in the Jordan. Some have even concluded that the Gospels are really "passion narratives with an extended preface." I think this is an overstatement, but it does point to an important truth.[†] We are told just enough about Jesus and his message that we can properly contextualize his sufferings, death, and resurrection.

In early Christian preaching and teaching, the death and resurrection of Jesus were at center stage (e.g., Acts 2:22–36). His impending sufferings weighed heavily upon him, especially during the later stage of his public life (e.g., Mark 8:31). Although Jesus' disciples could not understand the meaning of his words in this regard, they later found the supreme meaning of Christ in their fulfillment.

The meaning of Christ's sufferings and death is, within the New Testament, multifaceted. Jesus speaks of his death as a "ransom." This suggests the human family is in bondage to evil forces and a price must be paid to set them free. Elsewhere Christ's passion is described as a model of obedience and love. We are called to walk "in his steps," Peter wrote (1 Pet. 2:21). We also find significant texts that speak of Christ's death as an expiatory, substitutionary sacrifice. "Behold, the lamb of God who takes away the sins of the world," is likely, in part at least, an allusion to the scapegoat that, on the Day of Atonement, was symbolically sent outside the Israelite camp carrying away their sins (John 1:29).

---

†   N.T. Wright's various writings, especially *Jesus and the Victory of God* (London: SPCK Publishing, 1996), make a powerful case that the entire life of Christ is indispensably important and that exclusive focus on the passion narratives to the neglect of the rest of the Gospels is a tragic mistake. As a whole, I find Wright's approach to the Gospels not only compelling but also profoundly insightful.

No matter which of these approaches to explaining the meaning of Christ's passion we focus upon, the supreme underlying motive is *love*: "God so *loved* the world that he *gave* his only begotten Son" (John 3:16). *Love* manifests itself in giving. Love is motivated by the good of another and therefore acts with that goal in mind. Love is the heart of the Christian proclamation, then, and should bathe all the truths about Christ in its light.

Once we discover that *love* is the underlying motivation behind the salvation God showers upon the world through Christ, it also becomes the interpretive key to the rest of theology. Consider the problem of *Creation*, for instance. If it is true that God is supremely perfect in himself, Creation becomes a problem. Why would God create if Creation adds nothing to his perfections? God has no greater happiness on account of creating than if he had chosen not to create. It is not as if God is "lonely" and then chooses to create so he will have some company. This would make God dependent on the creation for his perfections. It may be the case that God *eternally* chose to create the world, a conclusion necessitated by his immutability, but there is nothing about the nature of God that required that he make such a choice. We may speak of God's eternal *free* choice to create but not an eternal *necessary* choice to create. The question then presents itself: *why did God create?*

The only reasonable answer I know is that God chose to create the world as an act of love. God chose to make a world, including rational creatures capable of love and knowledge, *for their benefit*. God's supreme life of perfection and love *overflowed* for the good of the creatures made by him. The world, then, proceeded from God by a free, creative act motivated by love.

This conclusion also yields further insight into our condition in this world. Since we have been made by God's free choice and love, we also discover that we are called to re-turn to God by way of modeling these perfections. We must return to God in freedom and in love.[†] Since our freedom is imperfect, it allows for a movement away from our true happiness only really found in returning to God. The story of the Old and New Testaments (not to mention the story of our own lives) is one of tragic rebellion. We have chosen to use our freedom and longing for happiness to find fulfill-ment in something other than God. This delusion leads to ruin—a fact seen throughout the tragedies, both small and great, that litter the course of history.

God's love did not end with creation, however. The sto-ry of Christ is one of supernatural love, a love that reaches beyond the initial gift of creation toward the life of grace. Through Christ, God restores us to the path of return. All of Creation, then, comes from God by a free act of love, and returns to God freely and by love on account of Christ who, by his sufferings and resurrection has poured out di-vine grace and love enabling us to find the original good intended by the Creator.

It must be emphasized that this love expressed in Christ originates in God: "*God* so loved the world (John 3:16)." John elsewhere states, "*God is love*" (1 John 4:8). It belongs to God's nature, then, to love. Love, though, requires an-other to whom it may give itself. A solitary person is capable of loving only itself. Self-love is certainly real. It is not the highest love, however. The highest love requires another.

---

† This theme of *exit and return* is commonly recognized as the underlying framework of St. Thomas Aquinas's *Summa Theologiae*. In part one he focuses on God and the procession of creatures from God (angels, material creation, and man). In the second part he focuses on the return of creatures to God by focusing on the human "end" and virtues/vices. In the third part he focuses on Christ and the means of grace in order to show how fallen man may complete the return to God.

The Trinity is an affirmation that, within the one God, there is truly subject-object relationship. Since the Father, Son, and Holy Spirit stand in *personal* relationship with each other (unlike the aspects of our mind) they are in an eternal and inseparable communion of love. This fact is seen when we focus on the analogy discussed in the prior section. The Son is the *full* gift of the Father's essence. The Father, then, fully gives his essence to a second, and that self-gift is the Son. This is the essence of love: giving one's self for another. The Holy Spirit, we understand, is the love of the Father and Son jointly sent and proceeding.

In human experience, we often discover that the love of a husband and wife is deepened profoundly by the addition of a third member: a child. The parents are then called to direct their love jointly toward a third. This requires a new perspective, a new kind of generosity.[†] Perhaps this fact sheds some light on love's meaning, as it exists within God. We discover the Father giving himself fully, and that is the Son, the perfect expression of the Father. The Father and Son turn their mutual love outward, and that is the Spirit that dynamically proceeds forth from them.

These observations reveal truths about God that are entirely different from what we would expect, given the history of religions. The contemporary religions around the time of the formation of both testaments featured gods of a very different sort. These gods, at best, were uninterested in humans. The best that humans could hope is that their chosen god would gain the upper hand in battle against rival gods. The gods of the Greeks and Romans notoriously disregarded the good of human beings in favor of their own self-centered ambitions. The supreme "moment" in the description of these gods was found in feats of power.

† This insight is owed to Richard of St. Victor's (d. 1173) treatise *On the Trinity*.

When the God of Scripture enters human history in his supreme "moment," he is not seen throwing lightning bolts off a mountain, nor is he found engaging in self-indulgent acts in pursuit of cosmic power, pleasure, and fame. Instead, the supreme act of divine "power" is found on the cross. The God of the universe chose to descend to lowly matter and then die among the lowest of social outcasts and criminals. No greater love has ever been known.

The Christian message is that this supreme act of love, unparalleled in all of history, reveals the inner life of God himself. What was made evident two thousand years ago was nothing less than what has always existed within God. The Father, Son, and Holy Spirit perfectly and unchangingly exist in a communion of self-giving love that is expressed on the cross.

Far from being a dull and dry belief, I do not know of a truth that more "excites" my mind and heart than this one. I do not know of a truth that is more meaningful in providing a foundation for our moral lives. I do not know of a truth more meaningful in my experience of worship. In fact, on numerous occasions I have stated that the greatest reason why I am a Christian today is because of the Trinity. I do not know of a more wonderful and life-changing truth than that God is a communion of love that expressed that love in history through Christ. These facts also define the essence of our future hope. The Christian journey culminates in a share in this eternal communion of love within the life of the God who is Love.†

Baptism, that sacramental act that initiates persons into the communion of faith in the God who is Love, plunges

---

† The resurrection of Christ, too, is an expression of God's love. Since Christ's resurrection is a foretaste of the general resurrection at the end of history, it is our guarantee that God's love for us will raise us from death to everlasting life; hence, everlasting love in union with God and the saints is the essence of our hope.

us into the life of faith, hope, and love that leads to unending union with Father, Son, and Holy Spirit. Joy should
fill our hearts, then, when we hear those words: "I baptize
you in the name of the Father, and of the Son, and of the
Holy Spirit."

In light of the discoveries of this chapter, I could no longer remain in the Oneness movement. Now the faith I once
rejected as "ugly" was the most wonderful of all truths. I
had no idea, though, that this discovery was a vital step in
leading me into the Catholic Church.

3

"Speaking in Tongues" and the Spirit Baptism

Pentecostal theology grows from a deep human desire to have indisputable "evidence," not only of the reality of God active in the world but also for personal evidence that God cares for *me*. Before tackling this very common human impulse as it appears within Oneness Pentecostalism, I'd like to offer some reflections on my experience as a Catholic to some of those who struggle with similar impulses. The Oneness understanding of "speaking in tongues" will undoubtedly strike most Catholic and even Protestant readers as bizarre. Perhaps the following reflections will help contextualize their teachings within the common struggle to live the life of Christian faith in our challenging times.

For more than two decades I have taught theology and philosophy to high school and college students. In many ways, my spiritual journey has been significantly different from theirs. Most of them have not grown up in anything remotely similar to a Pentecostal religious experience. The majority have grown up in Catholic homes, often in very devout families but infrequently in ones that spend a lot of energy questioning and exploring tough theological questions.

Because of the difference between my own experience and theirs, I have made it a habit for a number of years to administer a questionnaire to my students on the first day of a new class. Their responses, in part, help inform the topics I will select for that class. Always included among the questions I ask are: "What are the questions about the Catholic faith that bother you the most? What challenges do you have with believing the Catholic faith?" I was initially somewhat surprised to find that their answers consistently fell into one of several categories. First, about a third to a half of their questions focus on the problem of evil and suffering in the world. Why does a world like this exist if there is a good God that made it all? Second, another third of the questions are some variation of the following: "Why can't I see God? What is the scientific proof for God's existence? What is the cause of God? Why aren't prayers answered?" I put these in the same category because they grow from the same root. God often doesn't seem to respond the way that people expect, and the current climate of our culture emphasizes empirical evidence as considered by the scientific method as the only acceptable way in which to show that something is "true." The young people that I regularly teach find themselves in a difficult intellectual situation when they are taught on the one hand the scientific method, and on the other they are asked to believe in things they cannot see or that cannot be demonstrated the way that certain scientific conclusions can apparently be demonstrated.

The third category of responses I get from students is a variety of questions that focus on specific claims of our faith they find hard to understand or even contradictory. Typical among these is the Trinity (*How can God be both one and three?*), Christ (*How can Jesus be both God and man?*), the Eucharist (*How can Christ be present in many places at one time?*

I can't see Jesus. All I see is bread and wine.), and various questions about the Bible, hell, morality, etc.

Each of these categories is worth a book or many books. Here I will only suggest the initial path I will propose to my students when engaging these issues. The goal of these brief considerations is to point to the kind of "evidence" we can expect to support our faith and what we cannot expect and what this implies about how God works with human beings in our world.

With regard to suffering and evil, I tell stories of my own immature way of dealing with the suffering of other people when I was a younger man. I tended to propose rational solutions to painful experiences that people endured. For example, I recall a Oneness Pentecostal professor of mine who showed up late for class one morning. He was typically a well-dressed, punctual, clean-shaven man. This particular morning he was disheveled and unshaven. He proceeded to explain that, being a volunteer police chaplain, he had been called out early in the morning to the home of a woman whose son had just committed suicide. After identifying himself as a chaplain, the mother began screaming at him: "Why did God let this happen?" My professor then stopped his story and asked the class how we would have responded to her. I quickly raised my hand and answered, "I think this is an unfair question. The man took his own life using his freedom. God was not responsible for it." My professor was disappointed and even angry with me. "Do you mean to tell me that you would tell this suffering woman that her question is unfair?" I have never forgotten that moment. In fact, I regularly recall it when I think about suffering and evil in our world. What was wrong with my answer?

I long ago concluded that the main problem with my response was that it abstracted away from the realities of this particular person's life. She was experiencing something that could not be addressed merely by words or arguments. My professor proceeded to explain what he did. "I threw my jacket in a corner and sat on the floor. I told her, 'I don't know what to say. I just want to be present.'" His response to her was a deeply Christian one. Christ addressed the reality of evil and suffering in our world by being present with us in it and by sharing in the human condition. He shows us the power of love that ultimately triumphs over evil and death but not before traveling *through* suffering and death. The crucifix is a perpetual reminder that God is present with us in the mystery of suffering, a mystery that cannot be fully penetrated in our current condition. Even my younger students can often reflect on their experiences of pain, confusion, misunderstanding, and even deep loss, and find ways in which they have become more understanding, caring, thoughtful, grateful, and loving persons. There is an unsettling but profound way in which our lives are shaped and defined by how we respond to the unique collection of experiences that constitute our lives.

This is not to say that we cannot develop strong and compelling intellectual responses that address arguments against God's existence based on suffering and evil or other similar challenges. I certainly believe we can. My own experience has suggested, however, that it is most helpful to emphasize the love of God shown in Christ when people are most deeply concerned with these features of our world. If I start here, the rest of the conversation tends to be much more meaningful, and even consoling and persuasive.

What evidence do we have that evil is ultimately parasitic on supreme goodness and that good wins in the end? Indeed, there are rational considerations that support this conclusion. We also have our Christian faith that shows a moment in history that God enters our fallen world and suffers with us, triumphing over all in resurrection. We also have our own journeys that may give us windows of insight into God's plan but often in a way that is difficult to see, especially when we are in the middle of the darkness and cloud of suffering. Surely there is much more to be said about this profoundly perplexing aspect of being human. There is no collection of words, however, that can fully heal the pains of our losses. To be a Catholic Christian is not to have all the answers or quick solutions. Rather, we admit the deep sorrow and pain that sometimes challenge our faith. To believe in God in the midst of pain and suffering is sometimes to hold to a sure anchor when it is hard to see where we are going and even if we will make it to safety. The call to faith in the face of evil and suffering can challenge us to the very core of our Christian identity. With these thoughts I begin a conversation on suffering and evil.

Now to the second category of questions. Why can't we see God? Why is he seemingly quiet in response to our prayers? I have found it helpful to begin considering these challenges by questioning the naïve assumption that the scientific method is the only way to know that something is true. There are many problems with this assumption. For one, the scientific method is a way of studying certain aspects of reality that allow for the kind of certainty that science desires. It deliberately leaves out other aspects of reality that do not conform to the scientific method. In other words, science is so successful because it limits what it will consider.

Science considers things that can be quantified and subjected to repeated testing. Those things that don't fit nicely in these categories are not good subjects for science or, when science does deal with them, they look strangely dissimilar to what we consider them in normal experience. For instance, it is hard to speak of a science of "history." We may consider some things in history in a scientific manner (e.g., the human need for food) but the specifics of history cannot be repeated or quantified as such. How can one reduce a Martin Luther King, Jr., Martin Luther, Mother Teresa, or John Paul II to an experiment in a lab or a quantifiable entity? Their unique responses to history in their times result in historical peculiarities, not repeatable and quantifiable objects. How does science study "love"? Only in a very clumsy way that bears very little resemblance to our interior experience. Science focuses on third-person verifiable features of our experience, but leaves out the first-person aspects of reality.

There are many other problems with a "science only" approach to things. Science depends on a variety of assumptions that cannot be demonstrated by the scientific method itself. Inductive logic, deductive logic, the trustworthiness of sense experience, that the future and past resemble the present, and various other assumptions are not testable as such by the scientific method but must be used and assumed by it.

When we speak of God, we are not talking about an object that can be tested in a lab. Further, we are not talking about a quantifiable feature of the world around us. God is the very reason why there is a world. God is not an entity within and subject to time and space, but is the origin of time and space. Historically, most people have found the existence of God convincing based on the way they experience the world. Things are coming and going, including ourselves. Things that come and go do so because they are caused or moved by other things. That God is the reason for a world of things that depend on other things makes sense to most people, at least historically considered. An endless series of things that don't fully explain themselves results in an endless series of incomplete answers that do really satisfy our minds.[†]

What is the cause of God? The question is incoherent, when you stop to think about it. If God is the ground of all incomplete explanations and is the final, self-explained reason for them all, to ask about the cause of God is to put God back into the category of dependent effects that need a cause beyond themselves. That is precisely what God is not.

Why doesn't God answer my prayers the way I want him to? There are verses of Scripture that suggest that, if we ask, God will answer. I grew up hearing preachers preach about how God wants to heal everyone, if we would just have enough faith. They talked about how God regularly speaks to us and, again, if we would only have enough faith we could "move mountains." What are we to make of these claims in light of our lived experience?

The people who listened to Jesus talk about prayer were people who knew well a long history largely made up of

---

[†] My own mind tends to gravitate toward "cosmological" reasoning when I discuss the reasonable grounds for belief in God. This is likely because of my own childhood experience of the mystery that things that don't have to exist actually do exist. There are various other intriguing lines of reasoning that lead to the same conclusion, however. C.S. Lewis's version of the moral argument in *Mere Christianity*, Book 1, is quite elegant and compelling. The famous "Five Ways" of St. Thomas Aquinas are nicely explained and defended against contemporary challenges in Edward Feser's book, *Aquinas: A Beginner's Guide* (London: Oneworld Publications, 2009). This book is the best introduction to Aquinas's philosophical thought that I know. Reginald Garrigou-Lagrange's work, *God: His Existence and His Nature* (Freiberg, Germany: Herder Book Co., 1934) is the most compelling and thorough defense of Aquinas's arguments for God's existence and attributes I recall reading. Etienne Gilson's work, *The Christian Philosophy of Saint Augustine* (New York: Vintage Books, 1960) features a beautiful presentation of Augustine's way of discovering God through the ascent of the intellect from the experience of sensory things, to the mind's discovery of itself, and, finally, to God. Michael Novak's very stimulating and moving book, *Belief and Unbelief* (New York: New American Library, 1965), is rooted in the approach to God taken by Jesuit Bernard Lonergan. He considers the very dynamic of the human intellect toward truth and goodness as the soul's movement toward God. Robert Spitzer's *New Proofs for the Existence of God* (Grand Rapids, MI: Eerdmans, 2010) is especially interesting for those with a science background.

God's silence. They had waited for hundreds of years to hear the voice of a new prophet who would herald the coming of the Messiah. They knew the experience of suffering, foreign occupation, and persecution for their faith. Surely they knew the experience of doubt and confusion as they tried to make sense of the ways of God's providence. The psalms of the Old Testament include both expressions of joyful celebration of God's deliverance among his people and deep sadness and disappointment at God's absence and abandonment of the people. That Jesus promised that their prayers would be answered must have been comforting, but this comfort must have been understood within the context of the fact that God's timing is profoundly different than our own. They thought in terms of centuries and even millennia, rather than the fast-food and instant-gratification culture many of us experience.

I can point to some moments in my life when I sincerely believed that God was profoundly present and providentially directing and guiding my path. Some years ago I found myself in a very dark and confusing place in life. Some days I traveled to work with tear-filled eyes trying to make sense out of a very confusing and intractable set of challenges. Without describing the details, a series of unexpected "coincidences" resulted in a radical solution to these challenges that were so intricate, unexpected, and life-giving that I cannot help but conclude that God was present solving a set of problems I could not solve. In retrospect, I see those events as a kind of personal "Exodus" experience. Just as the ancient Israelites experienced God's solution to their long period of suffering, my own experience seemed like a deliverance that was hard to interpret as anything less than God's work.

Most of life is not like that, however. Most of life seems to be like the experience of the Israelites in the desert for forty years or even while enslaved in Egypt. The life of faith is often one that is experienced in a desert. We journey along, experiencing the provisions of God, but at the same time we experience a silence in which we are challenged to trust in God and focus on his acts of deliverance, and to keep moving forward or, unfortunately, to interpret God's silence in another way.

Does God answer prayer? Indeed, he does. Our knocking and asking may be a lifetime of knocking and asking, however. Prayer is a perpetual act of faith or trust in God, and we cannot dictate to God the terms of his answers. God often does not answer the way we want, because God is teaching us that we do not dictate to God what he will do. Our prayers are answered as they are conformed to God's will. Prayer is as much an act of submitting our will to God's will as it is requesting that God hear our request: "Thy kingdom come, they will be done." Prayer is, in the final analysis, the gradual process of realizing that we are redeemed creatures who stand in the presence of the infinitely holy God. God's will is supreme, and mine is often silly, misguided, self-centered, and prideful. That God does not do what I want him to do when I want him to do it is one of the ways that God teaches me that his work is not centered on me and that I have an awful lot to learn.

The third category of questions that my students mention is a collection of questions about aspects of Catholic faith that they perceive to be contradictory or lacking in meaning. I will not explore those questions both for sake of space, and because some of those questions are considered in other parts of this book. However, my approach to responding grows from the conviction that the Catholic faith makes sense and does not require that we commit intellectual suicide. Consequently, I feel an obligation to show that our faith is reasonable, and to offer ways to understand Catholic claims in a way that does not require that we suspend our rational faculties or accept real contradictions.

The questions that my students pose all have in common the fact that they are difficult and require patience, care, and determination in order to arrive at reasonable solutions. There are no fast responses that will satisfy a person who is struggling with those issues.

Oneness Pentecostals experience all the same human experiences that the rest of us do. I can remember praying for hours one night at a church prayer meeting for an elderly man in our church who was dying of cancer. I remember a young man, recently married with a young adopted daughter, who died of AIDS, contracting the virus through drug use in his youth. I recall an elderly woman who lost her husband and died several weeks later, apparently from a broken heart. I remember our pastor's wife was "healed" of breast cancer only to later have it reappear, and she died a few years after I left the Oneness movement. I remember a young man who was paralyzed from the waist down who hundreds of people prayed for one night at a healing rally, only to see him wheeled out, unable to walk later that night. Oneness people experience the same challenges of life that the rest of the world experiences.

Oneness Pentecostals, however, claim to have a moment in their lives when God miraculously proves to each one of them that they are forgiven and embraced by his love. This experience is that of the "baptism of the Holy Spirit." There is, it is claimed, a supernatural "evidence" of this experience: speaking in tongues. In the remainder of this chapter, I will present the case for this claim, and also show what I think are its problems. These introductory reflections, however, are intended to suggest that the life of faith is very different than what the Oneness Pentecostal pursuit of "evidential" experiences would suggest. There is a much deeper dimension to faith than a momentary experience that can then be considered the anchor of a life of faith. Instead, our faith is rooted in a deep conviction that Christ is God present with us in time and space. The darkness that sometimes enshrouds our lives reflects the nature of the Christian journey. We believe that this darkness will be dispelled by the light of life and eternal love in the life to come but, for now, we are on a journey that requires a faith that does not demand a personal miraculous evidence but, instead, clings to Christ—who is all the evidence we need.

Background

The Pentecostal movement is, at its core, built on an *experience*. This experience is called the "baptism of the Holy Spirit,"† and its "evidence" is speaking in other tongues. "Speaking in tongues" refers to an experience during which a person speaks in a language that is unknown to that person. The cause of the experience, then, must be *supernatural*, since its sufficient explanation cannot be found in the person. While speaking, the person has no awareness of the *meaning* of what he is saying.

There is reason to believe that experiences fitting this description, at least in some respects, have happened occasionally down through the centuries. Of course, there is significant dispute over whether these experiences actually

---

† The terminology used to speak of this experience varies. The Bible uses a variety of terms that are understood to have similar or identical meanings: "filled with the Spirit," the Holy Spirit "fell" on them, "receive the Holy Spirit," etc. Pentecostals often speak of baptism *with*, *of*, and *in* the Holy Spirit. One must simply get used to this variety of terminology even though it may be the case in Scripture that these experiences do not always mean the same thing.

involve *real* languages or whether they are simply ecstatic speech that has never been spoken anywhere in the world (or angelic realm). It is very hard to *prove* unrecognized sounds are or are not a language unless someone happens to recognize the meaning of the words. Although there are some claimed instances of this, the vast majority of cases do not involve recognized languages. Real languages, of course, were recognized during the events recorded in the Acts of the Apostles, chapter two, when the Holy Spirit was initially "poured out" on the followers of Christ. The many people that journeyed to Jerusalem from all over the ancient world to observe the holy days between Passover and Pentecost recognized the various languages spoken by the power of the Holy Spirit. Hearing the "wonderful works of God" in their own languages made them willing to listen to Peter explain the Christian message.

The twentieth century saw not only an increased interest in the phenomenon of speaking in tongues, but an explosion of interest in various other spiritual gifts mentioned in the New Testament (e.g., prophecy, healing). Speaking in tongues, however, was the experience at the heart of the Pentecostal movement. The central place of this experience was virtually guaranteed by the way the Pentecostal movement originated. Tongues were not first experienced and then explained. A theology of tongues emerged, and then the experience followed. Let me explain.

If we take the accounts of early Pentecostalism at face value, the movement began in a Bible school overseen by Charles Parham at the turn of the twentieth century. This is not to say the movement does not have earlier roots; indeed, it does. Parham, though, would contribute the "initial-evidence" doctrine, a doctrine that gave a theological and biblical framework for the tongues experience.[†] After "discovering" this biblical doctrine, he and his followers prayed to receive this experience. They did, we are told, beginning with Agnes Ozman, a student at Parham's Bible school early on the morning of January 1, 1901.[‡]

Parham believed the revival of the gift of tongues accompanying the "baptism of the Holy Spirit" had an eschatological and missionary purpose. The reemergence of this gift in the twentieth century signified, for Parham, that the end of the world was at hand and the gift of tongues would expedite the task of worldwide evangelization. The gift would enable the most unlearned to be missionaries to foreign lands.

Time would bring some changes to this original vision. Although some tried, the gift of tongues was of no help on mission fields. The experience then became increasingly significant *for the individual.* The sign of tongues came to have the primary purpose of proving to an individual that he has received the Spirit baptism.

Parham and his followers claimed to have rediscovered the "pattern" of primitive Christianity. That pattern is as follows: (a) the New Testament speaks of an experience called "the baptism of the Holy Spirit" that is *subsequent* to conversion or faith, and (b) that experience is inevitably accompanied by speaking in tongues. The original "Pentecostals,"

[†]   The most thorough biography of Charles Parham is James R. Goff, Jr., *Fields White Unto Harvest* (Fayetteville, AR: Univ. of Arkansas Press, 1988). See also James Goff, Jr., "Initial Tongues in the Theology of Charles Fox Parham," in Gary B. McGee, ed., *Initial Evidence: Historical and Biblical Perspectives on the Pentecostal Doctrine of Spirit Baptism* (Peabody, MA: Hendrickson Pub., 1991).

[‡]   Goff, *Fields White Unto Harvest,* 67-69. It is worth noting that Parham accepted a wide variety of "unorthodox" ideas, many of which were rejected by the movement (e.g., British-Israelianism, annihilation of the wicked). Parham fell out of favor with the movement he started on account of charges of immorality for which he was jailed but never placed on trial.

then, so-called because the initial appearance of tongues was on the day of Pentecost, believed they had recovered a missing part of the Christian faith. They did not, however, think their discovery meant only those that have spoken in tongues were truly Christians. It did mean that most Christians had missed out on an experience of empowerment that aids in achieving the purposes of the Christian church.

From a Catholic perspective, there is nothing surprising about the idea of *subsequence* or that the Holy Spirit, in some meaningful sense, is received *after* the life of grace and faith has begun. *Confirmation* is the sacramental reception of the Spirit imparted, normally, through the hands of the bishop. The classic biblical text used in support is Acts 8 where the Holy Spirit is imparted through the apostles' hands *after* baptism. Pentecostalism, however, sees no essential link between the laying on of hands and the gift of the Spirit. At least one similarity, though, is the notion that this is a *distinct moment* in the Christian life from the initial experience of what Catholic theology calls sanctifying grace.†

The Oneness movement, since it originated within the Assemblies of God, the largest of the classical Pentecostal denominations, inherited the initial-evidence doctrine. In other words, its leaders accepted the idea that there is a recognizable, distinct experience called the *Spirit baptism* and the evidence of this experience is speaking in tongues. Where they differed, however, was in the importance and meaning given to the experience.

Unlike the rest of the movement, the Oneness adherents believed that both water baptism (in Jesus' name) *and* Spirit

---

† "Sanctifying" grace places one into the sphere or context of a right relationship toward God. "Actual" grace is the power given by God in every particular act we do that is pleasing to God.

baptism are *essential* to "full salvation." It must be admitted that some in the early movement continued to believe that an individual could be "converted" and, therefore, stand in a positive relationship toward God *before* the experience of Spirit baptism, but the stronger elements in the movement thought otherwise. The Spirit baptism, with tongues, was an essential part of initial *conversion*. Bernard, for instance, concludes his discussion of this subject by identifying the Spirit baptism with the "birth of the Spirit" mentioned by Jesus (John 3:5).[30] You might recall, Jesus stated it is essential that one is born of "water and of the Spirit" in order to enter the kingdom of God. The implication is clear. If one does not have this experience, he is not fully a Christian and cannot be confident of going to heaven. This is, without doubt, the conviction I learned and professed during my years within the Oneness movement.[†]

In this chapter we will consider two questions. First, is speaking in tongues the initial evidence of the Spirit baptism? Second, what is the "baptism with the Holy Spirit" and, by extension, what is its relationship to salvation? By focusing on these two questions, we are not obligated to make a judgment on the value of speaking in tongues today, or whether or not this spiritual gift functions in the Church today. Although I will conclude the chapter with some personal reflections on my own experiences, these are not vital to the argument of this chapter.

The Initial-Evidence Doctrine

"I can prove to you that I've been born again. God made sure there was no question I'd been filled . . . I spoke in

---

[†]   My experience was primarily within the United Pentecostal Church (UPC), the largest of the various Oneness organizations.

other tongues, and that's the proof!"[†] These song lyrics summarize well the Oneness Pentecostal attitude toward speaking in tongues. It is a "proof" of salvation. "Tongues" is an essential part of Christian initiation and full integration into the local church. "Membership" in a Oneness church is typically automatic upon baptism, and tongues accompanied by attendance at a particular church. Often one hears the question, "When did you receive the Holy Ghost?" As long as one is unable to answer this question, he remains on the fringes of the local church.

Oneness Pentecostals profess to believe the Bible is the sole source of their theology. Given this conviction, it is incumbent upon them to justify their understanding of the relationship between speaking in tongues and human salvation from its pages. For all who are familiar with the Bible, it is apparent that no text exists that clearly states this doctrine. The twenty-seven books of the New Testament include three that mention tongues. Two of these are of no help in supporting the initial-evidence doctrine. The entire case, then, is built on a single New Testament book: the Acts of the Apostles. We will first consider the two texts that mention tongues but that cannot be used in support of the initial-evidence doctrine, and then we will consider the Acts texts.

The Gospels

The four Gospels mention speaking in tongues once. Mark 16:17 includes tongues in a list of "signs" Jesus states will accompany his believing disciples as the Christian message is proclaimed throughout the world. "Tongues" is given no place of prominence in the list, and I know of no Oneness

---

† Song written by Mark Carouthers ("The Proof"), music minister at the United Pentecostal church I attended in the late 1980s.

Pentecostal that takes all the signs in this list as necessary evidences of salvation or Spirit baptism. The other signs include casting out demons, picking up snakes, and drinking poison. It would seem most reasonable that this is a list of extraordinary signs that *may* be given by God as accompanying proofs of God's presence with the early Christian evangelists.[†] Further, it also seems reasonable that these signs will appear *as occasion requires them* rather than by design. We have no reason to think that the early Christians went about looking for snakes to grab or poison to drink. Similarly, there is no universal command or promise to speak in tongues. There is, then, no initial-evidence doctrine in Mark 16.

There is one text from the Gospel of John that is sometimes used to support the initial-evidence teaching. John 3:8, part of Christ's conversation with Nicodemas (a devout Pharisee and member of the Jewish Sanhedrin) regarding the new birth, focuses on an illustration of the "birth of the Spirit." Jesus insists that, in order to see God's kingdom, one must be "born again" (John 3:5). Nicodemas responds incredulously, "How can a man be born when he is old?" Jesus, seemingly on an entirely different "wavelength," expands his prior statement: "Unless a man is born of water and of the Spirit, he cannot enter the kingdom of God." This time, though, Jesus elaborates his meaning. He makes two major points: (a) the "new birth" does not originate in "flesh" or human nature but, rather, God's Spirit, and (b) this new birth is a sovereign act of God's Spirit.

In order to make the second of these points, Jesus employs an analogy. He likens the work of the Spirit to the wind.

---

† The prevailing opinion among contemporary scholars is that these verses in Mark 16 are not original. They are part of the "longer ending" of Mark that was, perhaps, added after the original composition of the Gospel. I will not assume this opinion is correct in this chapter.

The wind "blows where it wishes and *you hear the sound of it*, but do not know where it comes from and where it is going; so is everyone who is born of the Spirit" (v. 8). The wind is a mysterious force, and it does what it "wills" to do; in other words, it is not subject to the will of man. Man is not the cause of the wind's movements. The only way we know of the wind's presence is by its sounds, or *effects*. The point is clear: God *freely* bestows new life by the power of his Spirit. The presence of new life and the work of the Spirit are known by the *effects* produced in a person's life. In light of the rest of this particular discourse, it is most reasonable to conclude that the illustration has faith and Christian works in view (v. 15–21). In other words, new life is given by the work of the Spirit, and the reality of this life is shown by faith and good deeds: "Whoever *believes in him* (the Son) may have everlasting life . . . he who *practices the truth* comes to the light, that his *deeds* may be manifested as *having been wrought in God*" (3:14, 21).

Some Oneness Pentecostals have argued that this "sound of the wind" actually corresponds to speaking in tongues. The "sound" of the new birth or "birth of the Spirit," then, would be the first reference to the initial-evidence doctrine. Most Pentecostals, other than Oneness, do not make this argument, assuming such an interpretation ever occurred to them, since it would imply that tongues is essential to salvation, a position they do not take. Many Oneness thinkers do not make this argument either, for two good reasons.

First, the context does not mention tongues, and so the argument is highly speculative. Second, as mentioned, there is a reasonable and compelling contextual explanation of the "sounds" or evidences of the Spirit (i.e., faith and good deeds). "Tongues" is mentioned in none of John's writings, and so the use of this verse in that regard is entirely unreasonable and pays attention to neither the immediate context nor the broader context of the Gospel.

In sum, the Gospels mention tongues once, and that reference gives no support to the initial-evidence doctrine. If anything, that single reference supports the interpretation of tongues as an extraordinary sign, along with various others, given to Christ's followers as God desires to give them: likely in unusual circumstances.

The Letters

Twenty-one of the twenty-seven books of the New Testament are, broadly speaking, in the form of letters. Written to specific churches, broad groups of people, or individuals, these letters give invaluable insight into early Christian faith. Often these letters are prompted by problems, both theoretical and practical, that plagued the infant Church as it sought to define itself over against the many rival ideas and practices of the ancient world. These books, written under divine inspiration, continue to enrich and inform our understanding of the way Christian faith was taught in the beginning, and also provide an original model that should inform and enrich our own struggle to live and express our faith today.

"Speaking in tongues" is discussed in *one* of Paul's letters. No other New Testament letter mentions or discusses this topic. It is important to note that there are various letters that discuss human salvation (e.g., Romans and Galatians), but none of these contexts introduces tongues-speaking. The letter that does speak of this subject is of supreme importance, then, in coming to terms with the apostolic understanding of this phenomenon.

1 Corinthians 12–14 generally deals with the subject of spiritual gifts. Chapter twelve focuses on the purpose of spiritual gifts in the Church. Paul's primary concern in this

chapter is to show that spiritual gifts, despite their diversity, have the purpose of "edifying" or strengthening the Church. The *Church* here, as in every other place in the New Testament, does not refer to a building but *people*—in particular, the people that have become followers of Christ. Through baptism, we have been immersed into the one Spirit of God (1 Cor. 12:13). This union with God's Spirit also makes us "one," together in a single body. We are joined together with Christ who is now our "head." As our body's head directs and controls its various members and movements, so Christ directs his Church. The members of the Church, subsequent to union with Christ, are endowed with various God-given gifts that enable them to contribute to the "building up" of the Church. Spiritual gifts do not have the function of making one a member of the Church, but they do have the function of empowering its members to share in its support and advance.

It is in this context that *tongues* is mentioned alongside a variety of other gifts. Two indisputable points emerge from Paul's presentation: (a) *tongues* is one of *many* gifts; it is given no supreme or special place (in fact, with the gift of *interpretation of tongues,* it appears *last* in his list); and (b) everyone is *not* given the gift of tongues, or any other of the gifts (1 Cor. 12:7–11, 28-30).

Chapter thirteen continues the discussion of spiritual gifts, but here the focus shifts to something of greater importance. Unlike the gifts of the Spirit listed in the previous chapter, Paul focuses on something that everyone may experience: love. It is apparent that the Corinthian church had a significant problem with selfish pursuits of the more spectacular spiritual gifts. This prompted Paul's memorable words in this chapter about the supremacy and endurance of love. Speaking in tongues, he remarks, is nothing but noise unless motivated by love. Further, tongues, as with all the other "speaking gifts" (prophecy, words of knowledge and wisdom), will pass away. They are temporary inasmuch as they express divine truth during an age in which our knowledge is partial. Faith and hope, too, will pass away. When the *object* of our faith and hope is unveiled, all gifts and acts of faith toward, and in the service of, that supreme object will disappear and yield to the "perfect" reality and, hence, a perfect experience of that reality. The only "virtue" that will remain is love. Love will never pass away; it will only be intensified. Faith will pass away since it will be replaced by *certain* knowledge when we see Christ "face to face." Needless to say, this chapter, despite its profound riches, adds nothing of value for the initial-evidence doctrine.

Chapter fourteen is a somewhat complicated chapter. Paul lays down a series of observations and rules about how tongues and prophecy should function in the local church. It is fair to say that his supreme concern is that these gifts, as with all others, function in such a way that all can receive benefit from them. This implies also that these gifts functioned in a selfish, individualistic way in the Corinthian church. Those possessing the gift of tongues should not, Paul counsels, use their gift in the church unless it is accompanied by "interpretation," apparently a complementary gift that explains the meaning of the tongues speech. The central thrust of Paul's remarks is that speaking gifts should aim at *understanding*, so that all those present may receive benefit from the utterances.

A few observations are in order. First, Paul does mention that he himself speaks in tongues (v. 18). In the assembly, however, he insists that it is necessary to speak in a language that can be understood by the hearers (v. 19). I mention this text because it does suggest that tongues had some purpose outside the regular local assembly of Christian believers. Along the same lines, it is also evident that Paul never questions the legitimacy of the Corinthians' spiritual gifts. What he calls in question is their *use* of such gifts.

Second, Paul mentions that "tongues" is a *sign* for *unbelievers*, not believers. This striking claim is supported by reference to Isaiah 28:11ff.[†] In that context, Isaiah warned the Israelites of the coming Assyrian invasion. God would speak to the stubborn and unbelieving Jews, the prophet warns, by means of a "stammering lip and a foreign tongue." Since they had rejected the "rest and refreshing" that God had continually promised and offered, God would "speak" to them in judgment. The context is a harsh scolding and warning of devastation. Isaiah's point is this: since you will not listen to God's beautiful words of promise *in your own language*, a foreign people will overcome you speaking another language. Israel taken captive by a people speaking a strange language, then, has a clear meaning: Judgment has arrived.

Paul cites Isaiah's words and then explains that, if unbelievers come into their assembly and hear speaking in tongues, "Will they not say that you are mad? (1 Cor. 14:23)" If, however, unbelievers come into the assembly and hear words in their own language, they may be led to conviction, repentance, and faith (v. 23–25). In other words, if you speak in tongues, salvation will not result since the unbeliever cannot understand the message. He will walk away convinced that Christians are "mad" or insane. In this

---

†   Sometimes Oneness Pentecostals use Isaiah 28:11 as an Old Testament prophecy concerning the New Testament gift of tongues (e.g., Bernard, *The New Birth*, 221-222). It is confusing that he admits it may in fact refer to the Assyrian invasion (a fact evident from Isaiah's context) but that it has a "double fulfillment" in the New Testament gift of tongues. Given the pessimistic use of "foreign languages" in Isaiah 28, it is hard to see how it can have the positive sense Bernard gives it in his writings.

case, "tongues" has functioned only to contribute to the unbeliever's judgment, not salvation. The opposite effect is possible when a known language is spoken. The "sign" of tongues to the unbeliever is far from a positive use of this gift; rather, it is a facetious attempt by Paul to illustrate how counterproductive their use of this gift really was. Since the goal of the Church is to bring salvation to the world, the use of tongues in the assembly tends to work against that end, especially if it is not accompanied by interpretation. The clear goal, then, is to speak in an understandable way so that life and salvation may be imparted rather than judgment.†

Readers unfamiliar with Pentecostal theology may think Paul's teaching in 1 Corinthians 12–14 is sufficient to discredit the initial-evidence teaching altogether. Pentecostals do have a reply, however, to the apparent conclusion that all do not speak in tongues, found throughout the instructions of 1 Corinthians 12. Their answer is that Paul is speaking about a different function of tongues. Tongues had one function in connection with the initial baptism of the Holy Spirit and another function in the church assembly. Paul is writing about the second of these. Since it was assumed that everyone in the Church had the gift of the Holy Spirit, it was not necessary, it is said, to instruct the Corinthians about their initial reception of the Holy Spirit. Whether this reasoning is sound is a question we will have

---

† Bernard connects Isaiah 28:11 with the Spirit baptism since, after referring to foreign languages, that text states, "*This* is the rest and refreshing" (*The New Birth*, 222). This "rest and refreshing," he reasons, is the Spirit baptism. What he does not seem to see, however, is that if that text is referring to tongues in connection with the Spirit baptism and is used by Paul in 1 Corinthians 14 in reference to the gift of speaking in tongues, it follows that (a) all do not speak in tongues, and yet (b) all in the Corinthians' church had been "baptized in one Spirit" (12:13). In short, if we adopt the Oneness reading of Isaiah 28, the initial-evidence doctrine collapses by virtue of its use by Paul in 1 Corinthians 12-14. His comments on this text show no real attempt to engage the original context and Paul's way of using it in his letter. The "rest and refreshing" is not referring to tongues but, more generally, to the promises of God of final peace and rest.

to revisit. At the moment, it is sufficient to note that there is nothing in these chapters that will aid in supporting the initial-evidence teaching, a striking fact since this is the most extended discussion of this spiritual gift in the Bible.

In sum, the New Testament letters offer no support to the initial-evidence doctrine. Three chapters speak of this gift as one of many gifts given to people who already belong to the "body of Christ." The texts could not be clearer in stating that speaking in tongues is not given to everyone in Christ's Church. As noted, it is especially striking that Paul does not even allude to another function of tongues that applies to everyone in the Church. To the contrary, he insists that all do not speak in tongues.

The Acts of the Apostles

In light of what we have seen thus far in surveying the New Testament references to speaking in tongues, it is apparent that the initial-evidence doctrine is built *exclusively* on the Acts of the Apostles. Acts is the second part of Luke's presentation of the life of Jesus (Gospel of Luke) and the story of early Christianity (Acts). The two books of Luke feature a strong emphasis on the work of the Holy Spirit. Luke frequently mentions people that are "filled with the Holy Spirit" in both books. John the Baptist and his parents are "filled with the Holy Spirit" (Luke 1:15, 41, 67). Similarly, the early Christians were "filled with the Holy Spirit" on the day of Pentecost (Acts 2:4).

An examination of these texts, and other similar ones, reveals that the "filling" of the Holy Spirit is connected to outward manifestations of the Spirit's presence. Elizabeth, for instance, is "filled with the Holy Spirit" and "cried out with a loud voice" (Luke 1:41). Zechariah, John's father, "prophesied" when filled with the Holy Spirit (Luke 1, 67). Acts continues this pattern when it speaks of the disciples being filled with the Holy Spirit and "speaking in other tongues" (Acts 2:4). Not long later, the same terminology is used to describe the Christians that prayed and "spoke the word of God with boldness" after the Holy Spirit filled them (Acts 4:31).

All this talk of the Spirit of God "coming upon" and filling God's people is inherited from the Old Testament.[†] Numerous leaders of the ancient Israelites are given extraordinary power from God's Spirit to perform exploits in the name of God (e.g., Num. 11:17, 25; Judg. 6:34, 11:29, 13:25, 14:6, 15:14; 1 Sam. 16:13). In the many Old Testament references to God's Spirit acting upon certain individuals, the common feature is that select individuals, typically those in high leadership positions, are so gifted. The prophets spoke, however, of a day when the Spirit of God would be poured out "upon *all* flesh" (Joel 2:28ff). On the day of Pentecost, Peter applies these words to the events of that day (Acts 2:16ff.). Although speaking in tongues is not mentioned in Joel's prophecy, it does speak of miraculous signs (e.g., prophecies, visions, heavenly "signs"). Peter's words mean that the messianic age has dawned and God has proven this fact by pouring the Spirit out upon *all* the followers of Jesus, the Messiah. The listeners familiar with the prophets could not mistake this notion that miraculous signs will accompany the dawn of this new era.

In fact, the book of Acts begins with Jesus' promise to send the Holy Spirit upon his disciples (1:4–5). John the Baptist included the promise of the "baptism with the Holy Spirit" in his message (e.g., Matt. 3:11). Jesus assures his disciples that the fulfillment of John's words were about to find

---

†   For an interesting study of the Old Testament background to Luke's terminology pertaining to the Holy Spirit, see Roger Stronstad, *The Charismatic Theology of St. Luke* (Peabody, MA: Hendrickson Pub., 1984), ch. 2.

fulfillment. He also predicts that, after the Spirit comes, they will be his "witnesses" to all the earth. The advance of the Christian message is important: Jerusalem, Judea, Samaria, and the ends of the earth. This is precisely the pattern followed by the book. The gospel will be proclaimed first to those gathered in Jerusalem on the day of Pentecost (ch. 2). This faith will then spread to the surrounding areas of Judea (ch. 3–7), then Samaria (ch. 8), and, finally, to the entire world (ch. 9–28).

At each crucial moment that the gospel of Christ is presented to a new group of people, the Spirit of God is "poured out" or fills the people in some recognizable, miraculous way. After Acts 2, this fact is most evident in chapters eight and ten. Chapter eight relates the story of Philip, an early deacon and preacher who, on account of persecution, went to Samaria, just north of Judea, and proclaimed the Christian message. Although the Jews and Samaritans had a long history of hostile relationships, Philip was effective, and many received Christian baptism. When the apostles in Jerusalem learned of Philip's successes, Peter and John were sent to "lay hands" on the Samaritans so they might "receive the Holy Spirit" (8:15–18). They did. Although the text does not say exactly what sign(s) accompanied the gift of the Holy Spirit, it is necessary to conclude that miraculous signs were present since Simon the Great, a magician, was willing to pay money to have the same power displayed by the apostles, a power he "saw" (v. 19).

Similarly, in Acts 10 we encounter a crucial juncture in early Christian history. To this point, only observers of the Old Testament ritual laws were included in the Christian community. Both Jews and Samaritans followed the Law of Moses to some degree, especially with regard to the ritual sign of circumcision. In this chapter, however, we are introduced to a devout and God-fearing Gentile man who is not a convert to Judaism. Cornelius, a Roman centurion stationed at Caesarea, receives instructions from an angelic visitor and, in time, has the Christian faith explained to him by none other than the apostle Peter. Peter, as the story explains, is reluctant to preach to and associate with uncircumcised Gentiles. At this moment in Christian history he, and presumably all the Christians, felt a close bond to their Jewish roots and had no inclination to break with their customs and rituals. The events of Acts chapter ten will change this.

While Peter speaks of Jesus to Cornelius and his family, the Holy Spirit "falls" on those listening. What follows is astonishment on the part of Peter and those accompanying him since they hear Cornelius and his family "speaking in other tongues and exalting God" (10:45–46). Peter then baptizes this Gentile family on the basis of the divine proof that they were now included in the Christian community.

Acts chapter eleven relates the "fallout" of the events of the prior chapter. Peter defends his actions of baptizing an uncircumcised Gentile family, primarily on the basis of the fact that God had given them the same Spirit they had received "in the beginning" (i.e., Pentecost, 11:15–18). Later, the same argument will be used to counter the rising tide of the "Judaizers," those insisting on strict obedience to the Torah (15:7–11). The miraculous signs, tongues in particular, accompanying the gift of the Holy Spirit to the Gentiles, clearly had a profound effect on the development of early Christianity. Without such signs, there were elements within the Church that would have likely insisted on a closer theological bond with Old Testament rituals and practices.

There is one remaining reference to tongues in Acts. In Chapter nineteen, Paul encounters a group of disciples that associate themselves with John the Baptist. We cannot tell for sure what they knew or did not know of Jesus, but it is apparent that, at best, they knew very little. Paul's initial question to them was, "Did you receive the Holy Spirit when you believed? (Acts 19:3)." What prompted this question, we simply do not know. We do know that John the Baptist spoke much of the Holy Spirit in connection with the coming Messiah.† Perhaps Paul was concerned about their level of understanding the Messiah, Jesus, and wanted to know if they understood that the Spirit had already been given to God's people. These disciples responded they did not know of the Holy Spirit. Paul then asks about their baptism. Since the Holy Spirit is mentioned in Christian baptism, it was conspicuous that they admitted to no knowledge of the Spirit. After explaining the Christian faith, they received baptism, and Paul laid hands on them and the Holy Spirit is given with the signs of tongues and prophecy (19:2–7).

With Acts 19 we have reached the end of any direct mention of speaking in tongues in the New Testament. As already noted, the Old Testament contributes nothing to the matter of speaking in tongues, with the exception of Isaiah 28:11, a text cited by the apostle Paul in 1 Corinthians 14. That text does not refer to the miraculous gift of tongues but the foreign language of an enemy of Israel (i.e., Assyrians). Paul uses this text in order to make a subtle point about the need for meaningful communication whenever Christians gather together.

Formulating a Doctrine

The initial-evidence doctrine is based on observing a "pattern" in the information we have just surveyed. That pattern

---

† From this passage and others it appears reasonably certain that there were followers of John the Baptist that believed he was the Messiah. They must have continued in existence until well into the Christian period, as seen here. The apostle John also had to counter this belief by explaining the purpose of the Baptist's ministry (John 1:6-8, 15-27).

is simply that speaking in tongues is the initial sign that one
has been "baptized with the Holy Spirit."

It may strike some readers as strange that an entire doctrine necessary for human salvation is built on a single book
in the Bible. Oneness Pentecostals have an explanation of this
fact. First, they argue that the "plan of salvation" is not found
explicitly present in the Gospels since their purpose is to describe what Christ has done to make salvation possible. They
point *forward*, then, to what we find described in the book of
Acts. If we want to find how salvation is actually experienced,
we have to turn to the New Testament Church that begins
on the day of Pentecost. The letters of the New Testament, in
contrast to the Gospels, point *back* to the book of Acts. They
are written to people who already embrace the Christian faith
and need instruction on matters other than how to *become*
a Christian. The book of Acts, then, is the only book that
explicitly describes people in the process of becoming Christians. If the question we are concerned with is how to become
a Christian, the most relevant book is Acts.†

When we actually look at the book of Acts, we find people
having experiences with the Holy Spirit. Some of these are
initial experiences, and others are later experiences. This is an
important observation. The initial-evidence doctrine pertains
only to the *initial* experience one has with the Holy Spirit,
not subsequent experiences. This is because the "pattern" of
tongues speaking simply does not persist in all instances of people having experiences with the Holy Spirit (e.g., Acts 4:31).

Further, the pattern needed for the initial-evidence doctrine does not hold true before Pentecost, either. Therefore,
the "baptism with the Holy Spirit" prophesied by John the

---

† Bernard, *The New Birth*, 202–203: "The book of Acts is the pattern and norm for the
New Testament church, not the exception."

Baptist is unlike the acts of the Holy Spirit before Pentecost. On and after Pentecost, it is claimed that everyone who receives the Holy Spirit speaks in tongues.

In particular, there are five indisputable cases in the book of Acts in which people have some experience with the Holy Spirit *for the first time*. We have already looked at four of these (Acts 2, 8, 10, 19). The only case we have not considered is the conversion of Saul of Tarsus, also known as the apostle Paul. Ananias tells Paul that he will have his sight restored and "be filled the Holy Spirit" (Acts 9:17). No description is given of this experience, and therefore we are left to assume it happened but cannot make a judgment in any particular direction about whether or not tongues was associated with his experience. That is, of course, unless we can validly infer that he spoke in tongues from two facts. First, in the other four cases of initial experiences with the Holy Spirit it is either stated or implied that the people in question spoke in tongues. Second, we know from Paul's teachings in 1 Corinthians 14 that he did speak in tongues at some time (v. 18).

In reply, it is hard to imagine how 1 Corinthians 14:18 is of help in this case since, in that context, Paul denies that all speak in tongues but does claim that all the Corinthians had been "baptized in one Spirit" (12:13). These two facts taken together are incompatible with the Oneness version of the initial-evidence doctrine. The fact remains, however, that there is no description of Paul's "filling" with the Holy Spirit and therefore any proposed explanation of what happened at that moment is conjecture or inference from other texts.

With regard to the other four texts, it may be acknowledged that speaking in tongues either did happen or probably happened. The initial-evidence teaching is based on this fact. Since four of five initial experiences do mention speaking in tongues, and the other simply does not offer a description, we are justified, it is claimed, in drawing the conclusion that speaking in tongues was expected by the early Christian movement whenever people first received the Holy Spirit. Those who disagree with this conclusion are asked to explain what the evidence of this experience is, and offer a biblical alternative to the pattern expressed in Acts.

Problems with the Initial-Evidence Doctrine

I would like to present a series of observations regarding the initial-evidence teaching that will help to prepare the way for a solid evaluation of the strength of the evidence and argumentation described in the prior section.

Lack of Explicit Evidence

Perhaps the most important observation we can make is that this notion is not found in any defined form in Scripture itself. The primary reason there is so much disagreement on this subject is that there are no *explicit* statements in Scripture that give the Pentecostal conclusion based on the Acts passages. We see nothing similar to the following: "All who receive the baptism of the Spirit speak with tongues," or, "The baptism in the Holy Spirit is a distinct, recognizable experience from initial conversion," etc. These positions are based on inductive reasoning from historical accounts given in Scripture.

We should note briefly that this observation does not necessarily prove it is wrong. The doctrine of the Trinity, as discussed in Chapter two, is not found in a fully developed and defined way in the New Testament, but it is the *necessary* foundation for understanding what the New Testament teaches. A doctrine can be legitimately derived from inference, *but* we must be careful that we do not infer something that is not necessary or valid. It is interesting to note that

Oneness Pentecostals are quick to reject the Trinity on the grounds that the doctrine makes use of terms and ideas not explicitly found in Scripture.

The great difference between the two cases, I would argue, is that while the Trinity is the result of continued reflection on teachings that are found in the Bible, the initial-evidence doctrine is not derived from questions raised within the biblical text itself. The early Christians simply did not draw any conclusions regarding tongues that would require the formulation of the initial-evidence doctrine. The same cannot be said regarding the Trinity.

In sum, it may be said without fear of contradiction that the Bible simply does not articulate the initial-evidence doctrine; it is based solely on inference from descriptions of ancient experiences. We should consider the evidence for this doctrine, then, with the thought in the back of our minds that *the Bible does not formulate the Pentecostal conclusion.* Whether or not it is a valid formulation or inference from the narrative descriptions of various experiences is something we must carefully examine.

Misuse of Narrative Scripture

Second, the initial-evidence doctrine is based *exclusively* on historical narrative portions of Scripture. That is, the explicitly didactic (teaching) portions of Scripture have no bearing on the matter. In other words, the book of Acts simply states that various groups spoke with tongues when receiving the Holy Spirit. The conclusion is drawn that, because others had certain experiences long ago, our experience must correspond precisely to theirs. This is a leap in interpretation.

Furthermore, we must maintain that this kind of reasoning is dangerous. It simply does not follow that because God did something in the past that he will do so in the future in the exact same fashion. For example, God parted the Red Sea when the children of Israel were leaving Egypt and drowned Pharaoh's armies. Are we to conclude from this that every time God's people face a sea of water that God will part it? Are we also to conclude that in parting the "sea" God will also destroy our enemies? We may be justified in drawing meaningful principles from these narrative portions of Scripture (e.g., God will finally deliver his people, God's faithfulness to his covenants). This is a long way from saying that a particularity of a historical circumstance should be judged *normative* for future generations.

More specifically, it is evidently the case that we cannot assume the normative value of everything found within the book of Acts. Ananias and Saphira, for instance, fell dead when they lied to the Holy Spirit (Acts 5:1–11). Does this mean that all will die if they repeat the same sin? The answer must be "no," not only because this is a leap of interpretation but also because experience supports the conclusion that this was a unique happening. We would not even be justified in saying that God will kill every person who lies in the presence of an apostle since this would mean that we are saying God must always act in the identical same way. This is simply an abuse of historical narratives that are intended to *inform* rather than *prescribe* an essential pattern.

This is not to say that historical narrative cannot also prescribe a certain behavior. There are certainly biblical examples of narratives explained and applied to future generations (e.g., 1 Cor. 10:1–12). They are not used to prescribe specific divine responses to certain situations but *are* typically used to develop moral principles gleaned from prior historical events. This is significantly different from the initial-evidence doctrine that claims God will perform a specific miracle in certain defined situations.

Acts Narratives Not "Normal" Instances

The relevant passages in Acts (2, 8, 10, and 19) cannot be considered *normal* occasions. Furthermore, there are factors present in these passages that either cannot be reduplicated today or are generally not present.

In all four cases cited above, an *apostle* is present. In fact, when apostles are not present they are called *before* the Holy Spirit is received. This fact is especially interesting in light of the fact that in one of these cases Philip, a deacon, was able to perform great miracles (Acts 8). Imparting the Holy Spirit, however, was not one of them. Peter is present in Acts 10 after a series of divine interventions to get him there. Paul is present in Acts 19 and all of the original apostles (minus Judas, of course) are present in Acts 2. This is, at least, one accompanying factor that is not reproduced today. If the book of Acts is supposed to supply a normative "pattern" for the reception of the Holy Spirit, we should see apostles present. Oneness Pentecostals do not typically claim the office of apostle, however. Their ministers certainly do not insist on their personal presence in order to validate or impart the Holy Spirit.

It is difficult to see how Acts 2 can serve as a paradigm of receiving the Holy Spirit in all ages. Not only was the day of Pentecost the *initial* baptism of the Spirit, but that day also included a variety of other signs that are not claimed or expected today (e.g., tongues of fire, "mighty" wind). Additionally, those speaking in tongues were speaking languages that were recognized by the onlookers and actually became a means of attracting their attention to hear the message of Peter and the other apostles. From this chapter alone there are many other factors present that can clearly account for why God chose to use the sign of tongues on this occasion without resorting to a doctrine of initial evidence. The real question we should ask is, "Does the chapter *require* that we conclude with the initial-evidence doctrine in order to make sense of it?" If it does not, and here it surely does not, we are not justified in affirming it.

It is also worth noting that *none* of the people in these passages *expected* to speak with tongues. There is no evidence that any of them were instructed on "how" to receive the Spirit, or what to expect at that moment. In other words, in *every* case tongues was sudden and without instruction. Jesus simply instructed his disciples to wait in Jerusalem until the Spirit came upon them. When the Spirit did "fill" them, *all* spoke in tongues without prior instruction. Acts 10 and 19 are certainly sudden and without preparation. (This is true, at least, in Acts 10. Acts 19 gives no description of instructions other than regarding Christ.) Acts 8 is the only exception to this pattern, but really it is not an exception if it is seen that the Samaritans *immediately* received the Spirit when the apostles came to them. There is no indication of any exceptions.

From these observations, we conclude that if our desire is to be true to the *pattern* of Acts, we must expect an apostle to be present, and that no prior instruction or preparation regarding tongues be present in order to receive the Spirit.†
We might expand this list of criteria to include the observation that the Spirit always came upon crowds of people. When the sign of tongues is mentioned, we do not find the Spirit "coming upon" only individuals in any of these chapters. It is important to remember that these observations should not be quickly dismissed as incidentals to the

---

† There are numerous "how-to" books on receiving the Holy Spirit. J. T. Pugh, in his preface to his book, *How to Receive the Holy Ghost* (Weldon Spring, MO: Pentecostal Publishing House, 1969), writes, "For several years of my early ministry I found it hard to understand why many who sought for the Holy Ghost seemed to have difficulty in receiving that which was declared to be a gift." What is harder is figuring out how this fact is consistent with the "pattern" of Acts in which entire groups, without exception, spoke with tongues and without preliminary instructions or coaching.

situations. They are just as consistent as the sign of tongues. We must be careful not to disassociate what may be necessarily linked in the Acts narratives with the experiences they describe. These links may give insight into the purpose of the events themselves. It may be that the presence of apostles is emphasized in order that they may be unique witnesses to the divine acceptance of all groups of people into the Church. The emphasis is not on the individual reception of the Holy Spirit but the incorporation of whole groups into the Church (Jews, Samaritans, and Gentiles, disciples of John the Baptist).

Paul's Teaching

There is no good reason to separate Paul's discussion of tongues in 1 Corinthians from what we find in the book of Acts. This is a crucial observation since the whole Pentecostal position rests on defining different usages of tongues in the Bible. In other words, tongues as discussed in Paul's writings *cannot* be the same in function as what we find in the book of Acts. If this identification were made, one would have to conclude that all do *not* speak with tongues. All, however, are baptized with the Holy Spirit into the Church (1 Cor. 12:13).

We noted when considering Paul's teachings on this matter that he includes reference to the use of tongues outside the normal church gathering (1 Cor. 14:18–19). It is fair to say that the texts in Acts that mention tongues are not "normal" church gatherings. These are unique moments in the early history of Christianity. In fact, the first three texts (Acts 2, 8, and 10) describe the initial incorporation of distinct people-groups into the Christian faith. Even though the original meaning of Pentecost is that God intends the salvation of the whole world, and part of this salvation is a universal outpouring of the Holy Spirit, the miracle of Pentecost is extended in time in order that all major groups, Jews, Samaritans, and Gentiles, might *know* they are part of what began on Pentecost.

We do not need a miracle for us as individuals, however. Although I am neither a Jew nor a Samaritan, I know Gentiles have been incorporated into the Christian faith on account of Acts 10. Once every major people-group had experienced its "Pentecost," miraculous proofs were no longer necessary.

Acts Alone?

The Oneness Pentecostal focus on the Acts narratives to the exclusion of the rest of the New Testament is not persuasive. Keeping in mind that the New Testament as we have it did not exist in the first century, it is all the more disturbing that we can find a full description of human salvation only in a single biblical book.

Since many of the New Testament books were written before Luke's writings, it is striking they nowhere speak of the initial-evidence doctrine. We do find controversies about various aspects of salvation throughout the New Testament letters, but never a controversy or allusion to tongues in that regard. We are supposed to believe that a topic of such controversy in the twentieth century was of no controversy in the first. Additionally, there are texts that speak of the message of salvation "preached" by the apostles. For instance, Paul writes of the "word of faith *which we preach*, because if you confess with your lips that Jesus is Lord and believe in your heart that God raised him from the dead, you will be saved (Rom. 10:8, 9)." This confession of Christ has often been connected with baptism. As we have seen, profession of faith in Jesus Christ is part of ancient baptism (Acts 8:37). Paul assures the Romans that interior faith and its expression in baptism results in salvation. Elsewhere he says the same more explicitly: "You are all sons of God through *faith* in Christ Jesus. For all of you who were *baptized into Christ* have clothed yourselves with Christ" (Gal. 3:25–26).

Paul's summaries of his preaching, even though they are intended to clarify the meaning of Christ and reply to misunderstandings, never clarify the relationship of speaking in tongues to human salvation. The silence on this matter is deafening.

We might also add that the Gospels, too, are intended to lead people to salvation. John's Gospel explicitly states that it was written "*that you may believe* that Jesus is the Christ, the Son of God; and that believing *you may have life in his name*" (20:31). John's Gospel never mentions tongues. It certainly mentions faith, baptism, and the work of the Holy Spirit, but never is tongues linked to salvation, a major theme of the book. It is simply not convincing to claim that John left vital things out of his account since Luke includes them. The books of the New Testament are first distinct and independent literary units, and only secondarily should we consider their relationship to each other. We cannot be sure that John was even aware of Luke's writings. We certainly cannot assume that John's readers possessed a copy of Luke's books.

If everyone that seeks to be "saved" and live in a right relationship toward God should speak in tongues, it is astonishing that the New Testament nowhere asserts this fact in an unambiguous fashion, and the case for this doctrine requires a series of assumptions about "patterns" in historical narrative texts that pertain to the extraordinary days of early Christianity.

Do We Need Miraculous Proof?

Another underlying assumption of the Oneness Pentecostal doctrine regarding speaking in tongues is that a "proof" is needed that one has received the Holy Spirit. This assumption is profoundly at odds with the spirit of the New Testament. Those who have confidence in God, even though outward proofs are lacking, are praised in Scripture (eg., John 20:29; Heb. 11:39). The Oneness Pentecostal teaching would have us believe that every individual Christian must experience a *personal miracle* that "proves" that God has accepted him and given him the Holy Spirit. Nothing could be further from the consistent teaching of Scripture from beginning to end.

It is interesting to note that often miracles do not lead to faith. It was a short time between the parting of the Red Sea and the complaining, grumbling, and doubting of the Israelites. In the parable of the rich man and Lazarus, Abraham refuses to send Lazarus to the rich man's brothers to warn them of torment: "If they do not listen to Moses and the prophets, neither will they be persuaded if someone rises from the dead" (Luke 16:31). Miracles do not *cause* faith, at least not necessarily. Miracles may aid in directing faith to its proper object and may also confirm or strengthen faith. Those who refuse to believe, however, will persist in unbelief no matter what miracles are displayed before their eyes. Often those who believe solely because of a miracle abandon their faith when the demands of faith become too great.

We can fully admit and believe that miracles can and do take place today. We should also confess, however, that miracles are acts of God and are therefore done in the service of his will. Neither Jesus nor the apostles healed everyone they met. All illnesses were not eradicated from Galilee in the first century. Miracles, as we learn from John's Gospel, were *signs*. They directed attention to spiritual and theological truths that God wished to teach by them.[†] The resurrection of Lazarus, for instance, taught the lesson that *Christ* is the source of life (John 11:25). Our attitude should be one of openness to miracles, even in our own time. We do not *need* them, however, in order to trust in God. Whether or not I ever see an indisputable miracle, it is my duty to believe in God. There is no warrant in Acts or any other New Testament book to demand or expect a miracle in every situation of a particular kind.

There are signs or "fruits" that should provide a measure of evidential value in our lives, however: "No one can say, 'Jesus is Lord,' except by the Holy Spirit" (1 Cor. 12:3). Confession of the lordship of Christ is solid "evidence" that God's Spirit lives within us. There are various other similar signs that we should constantly cultivate and evaluate and thereby grow in the Christian life. These are of a different sort than speaking in tongues, however.

Death by a Thousand Qualifications?

The initial-evidence doctrine suffers from another problem. The doctrine requires so many qualifications—qualifications that are not specifically stated in Scripture—that we have to question the entire edifice. For instance, we must limit the scope of our study to a single biblical book.

Second, we must limit our inquiry to the period of time from Pentecost onward. This is claimed in spite of the fact that people were "filled with the Holy Spirit" *before* Pentecost (Luke 1:67). The Oneness argument is that there was a "unique" infilling of the Spirit after Pentecost. How so?

---

†   Oscar Cullman's book, *Early Christian Worship* (London: SCM Press Ltd, 1953) is a wonderfully insightful analysis of the Gospel of John's use of Jesus' miracles as signs of the sacraments.

The most we can determine from the biblical evidence is that the Holy Spirit is poured out on *all* members of the Church after Pentecost. It is the *same* Spirit and the same empowerment received throughout salvation history, however. Since people did not speak in tongues when "filled with the Holy Spirit" before Pentecost, we do not find a necessary pattern of tongues. We must *assume* that the nature of this "filling" (although the terminology is identical in the same writer's narratives before and after Pentecost) is fundamentally different. This is a highly questionable "qualification."

We must also assume that the "evidence" of the filling of the Spirit is different between the initial experience and subsequent "fillings." Why? They don't fit the "pattern."

All of these qualifications should cause some suspicion. Even though there are no post-Pentecost cases of people being initially filled with the Spirit where the text says they did not immediately speak in tongues, we also have no similar cases that state they did not prophesy. We *do* have at least one that says they did (Acts 19:3ff). Why can't we conclude that this is a second necessary evidential sign? Arguments for patterns from silence and from description are weak and rightly questioned.

We conclude, then, that the initial-evidence doctrine is not a valid interpretation of the New Testament data in regard to speaking in tongues. We can admit that speaking in tongues had an important function on the day of Pentecost, and on several occasions subsequent to that day. God freely imparted this gift, to the surprise of the observers, for his own purposes. If God chooses to grant similar gifts today, we certainly should not object. To insist that everyone *must* receive the same experiences described in the book of Acts, however, is neither accurate nor warranted by the data.

Baptism with the Holy Spirit

The work of the Holy Spirit, mysterious as it is, pervades the biblical teaching pertaining to the Christian life. In fact, the Spirit's work *precedes* and *enables* us to believe the Christian faith (John 16:7–11). The Holy Spirit convicts unbelievers of sin and judgment, and thus moves their hearts to faith. By his interior work within the mind and heart, the Spirit reveals Christ (John 16:13–14). We are enabled to profess the lordship of Christ on account of the work of the Spirit (1 Cor. 12:3). The Spirit's work not only brings a sinner to faith in Jesus Christ, it suffuses the Christian life and provides a "new law" that leads to true liberty. If we are "led by the Spirit," we are not "under the law" (Gal. 5:18). The desire and guidance to do what is truly for our good and pleasing to God arise from the gift of the Holy Spirit. All of life is understood in relationship to the Spirit's activity. If we "live in the Spirit" we will not fulfill the lust of the flesh (Rom. 8:4ff, Gal. 5:16).

Perhaps we may liken the work of the Holy Spirit in relationship to the Christian life to the light of the sun. The sun's light is crucial to "seeing" our way about in this world. It is also crucial in the warmth it provides to our planet. So, too, the Holy Spirit shines an interior light into our hearts that enables us to see ourselves for what we are, but also to see the overwhelming love that God has shown for us in Christ. Additionally, the Spirit, by his various internal effects, "warms" the soul and convinces us of the various truths that constitute the contents of our faith.

In light of these facts, it is very difficult to think of anything about Christianity that is not affected by the presence and power of the Holy Spirit.

Terminology

Our language about the Holy Spirit is, as with all speech about God, cumbersome. For instance, we must admit that the Holy Spirit, by virtue of being God, is present *everywhere* (Ps. 139:7–10). Or, perhaps more precisely, everything is present to God's Spirit. We cannot escape his presence. This fact seems to yield the conclusion that, since God's Spirit is everywhere, everyone "has" the Holy Spirit. This is not the way the Bible speaks, however.

The biblical writers, even though they are fully aware that God's Spirit is everywhere, typically speak of the Spirit's presence when some recognizable *evidence* of the Spirit is present. In other words, the Spirit is "present" when he is doing something that we can detect. If we were to see some miracle and later describe it, we might declare, "God's Spirit moved upon that person," or, "The Spirit of God came into that place and . . ." *We describe the presence of the Spirit in relationship to our recognition of that fact.* Sometimes called *phenomenological* speech, the point is that we describe things the way they are experienced or perceived. The Bible most frequently, but not always, speaks this way.

Everyone, then, does not "have" the Holy Spirit. We can speak of "receiving" the Holy Spirit in connection with certain actions of the Spirit that we identify. Since, for example, it is the Holy Spirit that places us into the Body of Christ and unites us together with the other members of the Church, we may speak of that "event" or moment in which we are incorporated into the Church as an act of the Holy Spirit.

The Bible uses other terminology. "Filled with the Holy Spirit" is a frequent one we have already observed. Paul encourages the Ephesians to avoid drunkenness with wine but "be filled with the Holy Spirit" (Eph. 5:18). The Greek text suggests an ongoing state of affairs: "be *continually* filled with the Spirit." Luke, as we have seen, uses this expression especially when God's Spirit empowers people who *speak out* God's word in some fashion. John the Baptist is filled with the Spirit "while yet in his mother's womb" (Luke 1:15).

This extraordinary fact is consistent with his mission as a prophet, a spokesperson for God. Elizabeth, John's mother, is "filled with the Holy Spirit" and *cries out* to Mary: "Blessed are you among women, and blessed is the fruit of your womb!" (Luke 1:41–42). Zechariah, John's father, "prophesies" when he is filled with the Spirit (Luke 1:67). Jesus, too, is "full of the Holy Spirit" after his baptism as he enters his days of temptation (Luke 4:1) and subsequently returned to Galilee "in the power of the Spirit" and began "*teaching* in the synagogues" (Luke 4:14–15). This brief survey of Luke's Gospel, by no means complete, shows that, to be "filled with the Holy Spirit" means that one is specially empowered by God to announce or proclaim God's word in some extraordinary way. This pattern continues into the book of Acts (2:4, 4:31, 9:17–20).

The Bible also uses the expression, "*baptism* with the Holy Spirit." Each of the Gospels speaks of this in connection with the Baptist's ministry. John contrasted his baptism with that of Jesus: "I baptize you with water for repentance, but he who is coming after me is mightier than I, and I am not fit to remove his sandals; *he will baptize you with the Holy Spirit and fire*" (Matt. 3:11). At a minimum, John was indicating that his baptism was a preparatory one. The "baptism" of Jesus would correspond to the fact that he was the Messiah and therefore would bring with him the messianic age, complete with a universal outpouring of the Spirit. The work of the Messiah will include, John declared, a power and presence of God's Spirit that would far surpass what happened through his preparatory baptism.

Christian Baptism

"Truly, truly I say unto you, unless one is born of *water* and of the *Spirit*, he cannot see the kingdom of God" (John

3:5). Here Jesus speaks of a "new birth" associated with the *kingdom of God*, Jesus' primary way of referring to the divine reality he was bringing into the world. This new birth is the effect of the Holy Spirit's work. We must not forget, however, that Jesus links the Spirit's gift of new life with water. Here is a vital Christian paradox: *spiritual life is given in relationship to physical, visible signs.*

The Christian religion, as discovered in Scripture, is never a *purely* spiritual one. Our existence in this world is *in union with* a body. We do not find life in God *in spite of* our bodies but, precisely, in and through our bodies. We "hear" the word of God. We discover love, not merely through intellectual contemplation but through the *acts* of love that we perceive through our bodily senses. We discover the reality of God, not by ignoring the data of the senses but, rather, by reflecting on the world as an effect requiring God as its cause. *The invisible is known through the visible* (Rom. 1:20). This vital connection between the visible and invisible "realms" not only explains why the Church had to respond forcibly to all forms of Docetism and Gnosticism,† but also why it insists on the normative reception of divine grace in and through sacramental signs.

The definitive affirmation of this fact is the *Incarnation.* When God wished to reveal himself most supremely, he united himself with a human nature. In and through that union, the first Christians were able to "hear, see, and touch" the eternal Word of life (1 John 1:1–3).

Before leaving this world, Jesus commanded his disciples to proclaim the good news of salvation to the world, "*making*

---

† Both Docetism and Gnosticism were ancient heresies that denied the goodness of matter and the true human nature of Christ. Docetists professed that Jesus only "seemed" to be a man. Gnostics, although varied in their particular explanations, held that the material world is inherently evil. Jesus was a divine messenger from the spirit world that gave secret "knowledge" by which the escape from matter could be expedited.

disciples of all nations, *baptizing them* in the name of the Father
. . . Son . . . and Holy Spirit" (Matt. 28:18–20). The work of
making disciples is connected most intimately with baptism.
Consequently, we find numerous references and allusions
to baptism throughout the New Testament. On the day of
Pentecost, Peter commands the crowd to "be baptized . . .
for the forgiveness of sins" (Acts 2:38). Paul is commanded
to be baptized "and wash away your sins" (Acts 22:16). Paul
speaks of baptism as a union with Christ in his death, buri-
al, and resurrection (Rom. 5:3–5), the internal "circumcision of the heart" (Col. 2:12–13), and being "clothed with
Christ" (Gal. 3:27). He alludes to baptism as the "laver of
regeneration and renewal of the Holy Spirit (Titus 3:5) and
the "washing of water with the word" that prepares Christ's
Bride, the Church, for the heavenly marriage (Eph. 5:26).
Elsewhere, Peter speaks of baptism as that which "*saves us,*"
as the waters "saved" Noah and his family from wickedness
in the days of the great Flood (1 Pet. 3:20–21).

It is hard to avoid the conclusion, then, that the New
Testament treats baptism as (a) the sign of initiation into
Christian discipleship, (b) the moment of the forgiveness of
sins and union with Christ, and (c) the act of "regeneration" or new life imparted by the Holy Spirit. At the root of
Christian baptism is the work of the Spirit producing these
effects. Unlike John's baptism, a baptism that *pointed to* the
Messiah and the outpouring of the Spirit, the baptism of
Christ would actually impart the Spirit. The "baptism with
the Holy Spirit," then, refers to the work of the Spirit in
connection with Christian baptism.

We should be careful to make a vital distinction. The
Bible does not treat this connection between water baptism
and the work of the Spirit as an absolute principle. It is a
normative principle, as we have seen from the various refer-

ences above. It is not absolute, however, as we may observe in the stories we have examined in the book of Acts. The most revealing text in this regard is Acts 10.

When the Holy Spirit "fell on" the household of Cornelius, the Roman centurion, those present began to speak with tongues. This occurred *before* baptism. This fact astonished Peter who then saw no reason to forbid baptism. He explained these events to the other Christian leaders at Jerusalem stating that, as he spoke, "The Holy Spirit fell upon them, just as he did upon us at the beginning. And I remembered the word of the Lord, how he used to say, John baptized with water, but *you shall be baptized with the Holy Spirit.* If God therefore gave to them the same gift as he gave to us also after believing in the Lord Jesus Christ, who was I that I could stand in God's way?" (11:15–17). Based on this remarkable text, we may conclude that the graces that are normally tied to baptism must have been given to these Gentiles *before* baptism. Of course, this situation is extraordinary. Baptism would likely not have been extended to them if not for an extraordinary sign. The sign of tongues convinced Peter and the other apostles that God had chosen to embrace the Gentiles, and that his choice to give them the graces of forgiveness and the Holy Spirit was his own, and not subject to normative rules and orders.

We must emphasize that it is not our job to determine when and if God will give these graces apart from their normal accompanying signs. It is *abnormal* for the Holy Spirit to be "given" before and apart from baptism. Besides Acts 10, there are no other instances of this in Acts (see 2, 8, 9, and 19). The "new birth" and the "baptism with the Holy Spirit" are typically "of water *and* Spirit" (John 3:5). Peter's instructions on Pentecost speak of "baptism," and attached is the promise of the gift of the Holy Spirit (Acts 2:38).

The "baptism with the Holy Spirit," then, is none other
than the graces of new life imparted by the Spirit in connection with baptism. If God chooses to impart these graces
without their normal visible sign, we may not object, but
neither may we determine these exceptions on our own.

The Bible does not speak of the "baptism with the Holy
Spirit" as the *end* of the work of the Spirit, however. God's
work in his new children has only just begun. God's Spirit
continues to empower ("fill") them to accomplish his purposes in this world. For this reason, we find people who
were "filled" with God's Spirit on more than one occasion
(Acts 2:4, 4:31; Eph. 5:18). "Life in the Spirit" suggests an
ongoing openness to the Spirit's work. Just as we may be
filled with a meal, and yet hunger again hours later, so the
infilling of God's Spirit suggests on ongoing need and desire
for new infusions of power and strength.

The texts in Luke's writings that speak of the "filling" of
the Holy Spirit, as already noted, are consistently tied to the
declaration of God's word. In other words, the Holy Spirit
fills people with the intention of making them public witnesses to God's truth. Indeed, Luke's writings emphasize
the evangelical mission to the world (Acts 1:8). One of the
primary objectives of the work of the Holy Spirit is to make
Christian believers into effective witnesses or heralds of the
good news. The other primary objective, of course, is to
bring new life, or salvation. The Holy Spirit, then, brings
regeneration and empowerment for service.

Just as the "baptism with the Holy Spirit" is linked to a visible sign, the waters of baptism (John 3:5, Titus 3:5), so, too,
the empowerment of the Holy Spirit for witness to Christ
is linked to a visible sign: the laying on of hands (Acts 8:17,
19:6). The laying on of hands is a rich biblical sign of *transfer-
ence* that reaches back early into the Old Testament: "Now

Joshua the son of Nun was filled with the spirit of wisdom, *for Moses had laid his hands on him*" (Deut. 34:9). Moses, the divinely chosen leader of the Israelites before his departure, imparted to Joshua the graces that God had given him to lead the people. The chosen apostles of Jesus, too, laid hands upon the baptized Christians to impart the same Holy Spirit that had been given to them at the beginning of the Church's history. Catholics call this special "gift of the Holy Spirit" for the purpose of service and proclamation, *confirmation*. These two signs, then, baptism and confirmation, are also sacraments inasmuch as they are also connected to divine gifts of grace. Both baptism and confirmation function as initiatory signs to a life characterized by the continual infusion of the graces that lead to forgiveness and service to God's kingdom.

In view of these observations, Catholic theology resists speaking of experiences of God's Spirit after baptism as "baptisms in the Holy Spirit." We may speak of them as "fillings" with the Spirit, but to use the word "baptism" blurs the distinction between the two primary works of the Spirit expressed in the sacraments of baptism and confirmation. The "baptism with the Holy Spirit," subsequent to the day of Pentecost, is presupposed in those who are "filled" with the Holy Spirit—recognizing, of course, exceptional cases (Acts 10).

This distinction also allows us to differentiate the tongues experiences of Acts from the "baptism with the Holy Spirit." It is true that Peter refers to the "baptism with the Holy Spirit" in his explanation of the events of Acts 10 (Acts 11:16). This is because the forgiveness of sins through the baptism of the Holy Spirit and fire (presumably fire is a symbol of purification) is a precondition for becoming a witness to God's salvation. Peter was able to infer the graces of the Spirit baptism by the presence of a gift of the Holy Spirit manifested before his eyes.

Conclusion

This chapter has considered two questions. We first examined the biblical case for the initial-evidence doctrine. We discovered that the grounds for claiming there is an inevitable "sign" of the Spirit baptism, i.e., speaking in tongues, are weak and unpersuasive. The Bible never states such a necessary connection, and the reasoning required to find it implied in the Bible poses a variety of difficulties, some of which were discussed above.

Second, we considered the biblical terminology pertaining to the baptism and infilling of the Holy Spirit. We emphasized the pervasive presence of the Spirit in the whole of Christian salvation, beginning before one personally embraces the truth of Christ. We also discovered there are two primary emphases of the Spirit's work that are expressed in Luke's writings (and also, in their own way, in other New Testament texts): new life and empowerment for witness. These two emphases of the Spirit's work are expressed in the sacramental signs of baptism and confirmation, signs that signal a lifetime of development and growth by the work of the Holy Spirit.

The Oneness Pentecostal theology of the Spirit baptism is unacceptable because it does not take sufficient note of the unique work of the Spirit in connection with baptism in contrast to the "fillings" of the Spirit in connection with witness or proclamation. The confusion of these functions, displayed by the Oneness refusal to grant that those who have not received the Spirit baptism as they understand it have not fully received the graces of regeneration, leads to the extreme conclusion that one must speak in tongues in order to have assurance of regeneration or the "new birth." The presentation of this chapter, brief as it is, outlines a way of organizing the biblical data on this subject that is not only faithful to Scripture but also to the ancient understanding of this subject expressed in both the Catholic and Orthodox traditions. We can do no better than conclude our biblical survey with some remarks of a noted historian of Pentecostalism:

> Amazingly, in almost two millennia of Christian life and practice, *no one* from the apostolic period until the nineteenth century—not even those who placed great emphasis on the study of Scripture—associated tongues with the advent of life in the Spirit.[31]

I conclude there is good reason for this fact.

Personal Reflections

Several years ago I gave a presentation at a parish about my journey into the Catholic faith. During the question period after the lecture, a lady asked my opinion about speaking in tongues. I explained my opinion on the matter. It turned out that she was very active in the Catholic Charismatic Renewal and did not think my evaluation was positive enough.

Because of experiences like that, I typically avoid evaluating contemporary cases of "speaking in tongues" and, rather, focus on biblical and historical issues. I would like to conclude this chapter, however, with some personal reflections on speaking in tongues so that readers may know my own conclusions about the contemporary Pentecostal and Charismatic experience of speaking in tongues. From past experience, it is clear that some people feel that a person is unable to critically speak about this subject unless he has personally had the "tongues" experience.

The first time I heard of speaking in tongues was in a large Charismatic church in Houston. The church called itself nondenominational, and the pastor was formerly a

Baptist minister who, after receiving the "Spirit baptism" with the "evidence" of speaking in tongues, left the Baptists and started a new ministry.

I was, if memory serves me, around twelve years old. I was standing at the back of the circular-shaped building on a Wednesday night, surrounded by literally thousands of people. I could hardly see the front of the building over the numerous bodies in front of me. Very moving worship music echoed throughout the building, and I could hear someone behind me uttering a smooth, unbroken series of sounds that I could not understand. I sensed that this was a spiritual experience of some sort but did not know what it was.

My limited religious experience to this point was with the Methodists and Baptists. During my earliest years, my family did not attend any church. When I was in early grade school, my parents sent my sister and me to a local Baptist church for Sunday school. Later, after moving across town, we were sent to Sunday school at a Methodist church. It was several years later that our whole family became involved in another Baptist church. This time our attendance and involvement was much more significant.

When I listened to this person "speak in tongues," I was not frightened or concerned in any way. I, too, was caught up in this worship experience. I had a strong love of God and the message of salvation through Christ. The vibrancy and sincerity of those involved in this church was deeply appealing.

Soon afterward, my mother began accumulating Charismatic literature. I avidly read all of it. One of these was a pamphlet on "speaking in tongues." It offered, what I would later discover, the standard arguments in support of the initial-evidence doctrine, the foundational distinctive doctrine of the Pentecostal movement. I did not personally experience speaking in tongues, however, until I walked into a Oneness Pentecostal church.

When I did finally speak in tongues, it was admittedly a powerful experience. I was overwhelmed with a sense of God's love. There was almost a tangible "light" or brightness all around me. I began to utter sounds uncontrollably. I did not know their meaning, nor did I care. My entire disposition was toward worshiping God, and I believed that these sounds coming from my mouth did just that. This went on for more than thirty minutes, and then I was taken, along with my mother and sister, and baptized "in Jesus' name."

For over a decade, I continued to worship and serve within a Pentecostal context. Seven of these years were spent within Oneness Pentecostalism, and five years within the Assemblies of God, a trinitarian Pentecostal denomination. Although I "spoke in tongues" numerous times (we were silently "expected" to do so on occasion), my initial experience was never duplicated. With very few exceptions, I am convinced that those other experiences were fundamentally different in nature than my first personal encounter with "tongues."

I also heard others speak in tongues countless times. It is fair to say that I have heard people speak in tongues thousands of times in a variety of circumstances. I have heard numerous "messages in tongues" followed by interpretations of those messages. I have prayed with numerous people to "receive the Holy Spirit" and speak in tongues.

It is also fair to say that I have read an extensive body of literature on this subject, both from those who are convinced members of the tongues movement as well as from those who are committed opponents. Since the tongues experience was an integral part of what made Pentecostalism unique, I felt an obligation to study it thoroughly.

Evaluation

My own personal conclusions may be summed up in the following points. They are simply a summary of major observations I would make based on my first-hand experience of the tongues movement. My biblical and theological evaluation has already been presented and need not be repeated.

I start with some positive observations. First, I do believe that the experience of speaking in tongues can be a meaningful spiritual experience for many. It can strengthen their life of prayer and worship and renew their devotion and desire to serve God and others. Second, I am open to at least some speaking in tongues being a miraculous gift from God. Third, I am also open to the possibility that some speaking in tongues is a legitimate spiritual experience but not, properly speaking, supernatural. Loss of speaking ability and uttering incomprehensible sounds may be explained psychologically in various ways. There are some significant studies in this regard.[†] Even though there may be psychological explanations of speaking in tongues, I don't think this necessarily discredits the experience altogether. It may simply be a human reaction, on a deep level, to the perceived presence of God. The history of religious experience is strewn with similar experiences. There are likely instances of such experiences among Catholic saints.

My observations would be incomplete, however, without a few, more negative observations. First, I do think that there is a significant portion of "speaking in tongues" that is neither miraculous nor deeply psychological/spiritual in

---

†   See John Kidahl, *The Psychology of Speaking in Tongues* (New York: Harper and Row, 1972), and M. Kelsey, *Tongues Speaking: The History and Meaning of Charismatic Experience* (New York: Crossroad, 1981). Kidahl concluded that speaking in "tongues" has many positive advantages for a person's spiritual and personal life (without endorsing it as a miraculous gift). Kelsey analyzes tongues through the grid of Jungian psychoanalysis. Like dreams, "tongues" expresses deep spiritual meaning but is more "pre-linguistic" than a real, spoken language.

origin. Some is mere "imitation" of sounds heard from others or simply produced randomly, much like a small child making up words. It was not hard to "learn" the sounds that some people used when speaking in tongues. They could reproduce them at will. I see no reason to consider these experiences anything more than a learned phenomenon.

Second, although speaking in tongues may be profoundly meaningful on occasion, I have not found that it continues in that role throughout one's Christian experience. Those who "depend" on the regular experience of tongues typically struggle with instability. I do not attribute this directly to tongues, but sometimes speaking in tongues becomes a psychological or spiritual "crutch" or gauge by which a person determines if they are "spiritual."

Finally, as Paul's first letter to the Corinthians suggests, speaking in tongues can be desired and experienced to the neglect of the far superior gift of *love*. Even if speaking in tongues is a legitimate spiritual gift, it is only one of them, and must be subordinated and oriented toward the truly enduring virtues. A great deal of spiritual immaturity can co-exist with the quest for spectacular spiritual gifts.

My own initial experience was indeed powerful. I cannot deny that. I do not know how my life would have been different without that experience. I had a strong desire to serve God both before and after that day. It probably "biased" me for a number of years in the direction of Pentecostalism. The Catholic Church officially allows the Charismatic Renewal to exist within its context. Catholics are neither obligated to strive to speak in tongues nor to oppose it. I suspect a wide range of opinions on this question exist within the Church. This diversity should not bother us greatly as long as "tongues" does not become a "test" of one's spirituality or orthodoxy.

In sum, I am not opposed to the practice of speaking in tongues if one finds it helpful devotionally. I also do not feel compelled to dispute with those who do not practice it in their own spiritual life. My deepest concern regards formulating a doctrine involving speaking in tongues that makes it normative for all Christians. The New Testament and Christian experience are opposed to such formulations.

Why Catholicism?

"He became a Catholic. The next step for him is that he will become an atheist." A friend reported to me these words that were allegedly spoken about me by my former Oneness pastor. The Catholic faith is so vilified among those of my background that to leave and become a Catholic is about as bad as it gets, in their minds. The only thing left after becoming a Catholic is denying God altogether.

I bumped up against Catholicism a number of times during my youth and young adult life. Most of those times I quickly moved on to something else with little thought. Based on what I had learned, the Catholic Church was a shell of original Christianity, and there was nothing about it that was attractive. There were some exceptional moments, however, that would give me pause.

One hot summer afternoon, my Oneness pastor asked me and a few other young men to help move a large number of books from his office to the church library. The church library was a third-floor room in the church. It was somewhat difficult to access. We spent a few long days carrying a large quantity of books to that space. Exhausted, I sat down on the library floor and began to look through some of the books that caught my eye. One of those books was entitled, if memory serves me well, *Introduction to the Sacraments*. The word *sacrament* was not in my vocabulary. I flipped through the book, glancing at sections that caught my attention. In hindsight, I'm confident the book was a Catholic textbook, probably intended for high school or undergraduate students. To my surprise, I saw verses of Scripture used to support Catholic teachings that I was convinced were simply concocted by Catholics out of thin air. I didn't pause long before putting it aside, but there was a brief pause. "So that's where they get those beliefs."

Several years later, I became aware of Chick Publications. Chick Publications was known for its anti-Catholic literature. Their small tracts and magazine-style literature were attractive, shocking, and effective. Among their popular materials was the comic book series based on the life of Alberto Rivera. Alberto was supposedly a former Jesuit priest who left the priesthood. He told a shocking story of the evils of the Catholic Church in a way that rivaled the most extreme conspiracy theories. I was suspicious of his story. Chick Publications published a book responding to criticisms about the veracity of Alberto's story: *Is Alberto for Real?* I read this defense of Alberto but found it unpersuasive. There was one piece of data that I did find interesting, however. One page in the book featured three pictures of "former" Catholic religious persons (one priest and two nuns), each of which is quoted as supporting the contents of Alberto's story. The only problem was that the information regarding the identity of these persons was so generic that there was no way to verify their stories or even identities.

Because this looked suspicious, I wrote to Jack Chick, founder of Chick Publications, and asked for further information about how to verify the stories of those used to support Alberto's story. After receiving no reply, I wrote an article that appeared in a Christian periodical criticizing the nature of the evidence used to support the conspiracy theories of Alberto Rivera. My interest was certainly not in defending Catholicism. To the contrary, I was simply reacting to a conspiracy theory that found its way into my awareness.

Shortly after the article appeared, I received a package from Chick Publications that included a letter signed by Jack Chick along with an old anti-Catholic book (Alexander Hislop's *The Two Babylons*). In his letter, Chick apologized for his delay in replying. He then informed me that I could not have contact information for any of those featured in his book. One had died, one could not be located, and the other worked for Chick's company but had no desire to correspond. Needless to say, I was disappointed. This experience, although years before I became a Catholic, caused me to look with greater suspicion on quick dismissals of the Catholic tradition. I was not prepared to become a Catholic, but I was moving toward at least giving the Church a fair hearing. "You'll find all the answers you need in the enclosed book," Chick wrote, in reference to Hislop's book. Needless to say, I was not impressed.

Shortly after leaving the Oneness Pentecostal movement, I wrote an article on the Trinity and the Bible. It struck me that those who reject the Trinity use and quote from the same Bible that trinitarians use and quote. Why do we have the same Bible? The reason is because non-trinitarian forms of Christian belief are historical offshoots of trinitarian ones. They came to exist because of a protest of some kind, but they are historically related. The problem, as I saw it, was that non-trinitarians accepted the Bible that trinitarians recognized, accepted, and passed along to them but don't accept the decisions that the same people made about what the Bible means on the subject of God. Why accept one decision and not the other?

In my article, I insisted that it is inconsistent to accept the Bible from trinitarians but not accept the Trinity. A Baptist minister friend of mine read my article and reacted with horror: "Your article sounds like what a Catholic would argue! You can't submit that for publication." His rejection bothered me because I thought my reasoning was sound. That I was accused of thinking like a Catholic bothered me. I put the article aside and did not pursue publishing it.

The coming years would bring an intensification of experiences that forced me to confront the questions raised by these problems and considerations. Could it be that my youthful insight into the inconsistency of anti-trinitarian believers also applied to me . . . unless I became a Catholic?

A Grave Problem

"Bro. Larry," the Oneness minister who initially explained to me the theological ideas discussed in this book, became a controversial figure in the years since that encounter. He came to disagree with the standard Oneness understanding of "end times" matters. Pentecostalism, from its beginnings, was very much an eschatological movement. With few exceptions, Pentecostals have strongly believed that we are living in the final moments of history and the Second Coming of Christ will be very soon. The Pentecostal denominations take their understanding of these matters so seriously, they often require regular reaffirmations of these commitments for retaining ministerial credentials.[†]

---

†   I held ministerial credentials with the Assemblies of God for several years and was required to assent to the belief in the pre-tribulation theory of the Rapture and premillenialism each year.

I recall my Oneness pastor citing a text from Hosea 6:2: "He (God) will revive us after *two days*. He will raise us up on the *third day*." He explained that "days" in the Bible are actually a symbol for 1,000 years. In this text, the "two days" actually mean 2,000 years, he said. At the end of 2,000 years, then, there will be a resurrection. The third "thousand-year" period of time is equal to the millennium, the period of time that Christ will reign over an earthly kingdom subsequent to his Second Coming (Rev. 20).

Somehow my pastor had determined that the first "two days" would expire in the year 2000. I recall him noting various events making news reports and remarking, "It's getting very close! We know that by the end of this millennium, Jesus will return." He would even announce, with Bible in hand, "If this Bible is true, this thing will all be wrapped up by the year 2000." He would often cite Hosea 6:2 in support of this conclusion. My pastor was not someone who would strike you as an imbalanced man. He was a dignified, respectable man who commanded respect; there was an "air" of authority around him. People did not question his interpretations, at least not to his face.

On another occasion, I recall listening to a dynamic and compelling Oneness preacher, a "specialist" in biblical prophecy, explain why the "Rapture" of the church had to take place by a particular date.[†] That was, as I recall,

† The "Rapture," or "catching away" of the church in a "secret" coming of Christ is professed by most Pentecostals. Most hold this event will occur at the beginning of a seven-year period of "tribulation" that will precede the visible return of Christ. The Rapture, then, is not the same thing as the Second Advent. Some hold the Rapture will occur about midway through the tribulation period, and others hold it will occur at its end. The Bible does speak of a "catching away" of Christians (1 Thess. 4:17) but, I would argue, the case for separating this event from the Second Advent is quite weak. The book that was most influential in clarifying my thoughts on this subject was George Eldon Ladd's, *The Blessed Hope* (Grand Rapids, MI: Eerdmans, 1956).

sometime back in the mid-1980s. His presentations were so persuasive, and the sense that Christ would return any moment was so real, people literally screamed in fear. I have never again heard such frightening sounds at a religious gathering.

Bro. Larry, from what I can gather, came to disagree with some of the "orthodox" Pentecostal notions of the "end times." It is needless to explore what he came to believe. He found himself under attack by his "brethren," though. He was convinced of the truth of his position. Apparently there were "prophets" that came to his church who confirmed the truth of what he had come to believe. He was also convinced of his beliefs because, he said, God, in moments of prayer, had confirmed them.

Of course, time has shown my old pastor and the prophecy preacher were *wrong*. Space is insufficient to tell other similar stories.[†] Their reading of Scripture must have been in error. These facts pose a nagging question that begs to be answered: if their interpretation of those portions of Scripture was in error, *what about other matters?*

Most Oneness Pentecostals are not "experts" in their beliefs or, more generally, in knowledge of Scripture. A good number of regular churchgoers display a respectable degree of biblical literacy, but the "average" member of a Oneness church finds it difficult to answer hard biblical questions about their own beliefs. Without doubt, this is true of "average" church members of any and every form

---

† Perhaps the most notable one is Edgar Wisenaut's *88 Reasons Why the Rapture Will Be in 1988: The Feast of Trumpets (Rosh Hash-Ana) September 11-12-13* (Whisenant/World Bible Society, 1988) Many in Oneness Pentecostalism and outside it accepted the claims of this book—a book riddled with atrocious interpretations of the Bible. My recollection is that well over a million copies of this book sold in the days leading up to the author's target dates in September 1988.

of Christianity. Most Christians have an *implicit* faith that accepts the "message" given to them, even if they have a hard time articulating that message. Much of the content of our faith is *inherited* and, unless some crisis appears, believed. Not only is this situation the way things are, it is *unavoidable*. Most church members spend their days working or going to school, taking care of their families, mowing their yards, washing dishes, cooking dinners, and a host of other daily tasks. Mastering the disciplines required to be an "expert" in the study the Bible is not only difficult for such persons, *it is practically impossible*. We may conclude, given the human situation, *God never intended his Church to be made up of Bible scholars!* Of course, some are able and willing to devote themselves to such studies, hopefully in support of the Church's mission. Most are not, however, and must live out the Christian life with a variety of other occupations. For most Christians, having a basic grasp of their faith, a general understanding of the Bible, and progressive growth in Christian virtues is about as much as we can hope for. Anyone engaged in pastoral work or teaching the Faith in any capacity will understand the truth of these observations.

It is hard to find a single person in any congregation of Oneness Pentecostals (or any other church) who can give a coherent sketch of the history of the Bible. The long and complicated path along which Scripture has been transmitted to us, thousands of years after its original appearance, is challenging indeed. It is nonetheless true, however, that Oneness Pentecostals believe, with great confidence, that the Bible is the word of God and is entirely without error. One would be hard-pressed to find a committed Oneness Pentecostal who would disagree with this statement. One would also be hard-pressed to find someone who would dispute the table of contents found in his Bible. The Bible, they would all agree, is exactly what it should be, no more, no less.[†]

There is a serious problem, however. If asked to explain *how* the Bible came to include the books it does contain, blank stares or *ad hominem* attacks frequently follow. If asked, for instance, why the Bible should not include the *Wisdom of Solomon* or the *Gospel of Thomas*, books they have likely never read or heard of, similar blank stares would appear. Oneness Pentecostals strongly believe in certain truths but cannot explain why.

That is, of course, unless we accept purely subjective arguments. One might say, "I know the Bible I have is God's word because when I read it God confirms it is true." I do not wish to dispute the confirming power of God's Spirit that may accompany one's reading of the Bible. This argument is often questionable, however, for a very good reason. Most Oneness Pentecostals accept the Bible as the inspired word of God *before they ever read it*. Most of them, as with all Christian groups, have never read the whole Bible. Further, they accept it as *inerrant* before they examine every instance of a supposed "contradiction." Indeed, if shown a "contradiction" they cannot explain, they will continue to believe the text is without error and inspired by God. I have never met anyone that claimed he *first* read the entire Bible and then concluded it was the word of God. Further, I've also never met anyone who read all the other extant ancient literature that appeared contemporaneously with the Bible (but was not finally in-

---

[†] Sometimes this conviction expresses itself in the radical belief that a particular English translation of the Bible (typically the King James Version) is a perfect translation and therefore no need exists to consult any other version or language. Often called "KJV Only," this theory results from a longing for certainty but avoiding the complex questions of biblical history and interpretation. I have encountered this theory among Baptists and Oneness believers.

cluded in it) and then concluded it should not be in the Bible. All accept these claims on some other basis.

What, then, is their *real* basis for confidence in the Bible's authority, inerrancy, and table of contents (i.e., *canon*)? Whence comes this certitude for which, I have no doubt, many Oneness Pentecostals would give their lives? *Their confidence arises from their trust in their minister, their personal experience, and the organized religion of which they are a part.* Their real "final authority" is not the "Bible alone" but the *ministers* they have come to believe and the personal experiences they have had. It is the minister who assures them of what the Bible is and what its nature is. The ministers, on the other hand, insist their teachings and claims are rooted entirely and solely in the Bible. They do not typically claim some God-given authority to interpret the Bible that, in principle, is not possessed by everyone in their churches.

Within the Oneness movement, one often hears references to "revelation" knowledge. Coming to understand the Oneness doctrine requires a "revelation." It is said, the difference between those who read the Bible and conclude it teaches God is a Trinity and those who read it and conclude to the Oneness doctrine is a *revelation* from God. Often this "revelation" knowledge sounds much like a *separate* source of information. In principle, Oneness Pentecostals do not speak of it as a separate source of information, however, since this would compromise their profession that the Bible alone is the source of their faith. In practice, things are often different. Frequently, assertions of "truth" are made in the face of biblical texts that cannot be reconciled with their claims. In spite of the fact that they are, on occasion, unable to offer a compelling reply to a question about Scripture, they persist in speaking of the "revelation" they have received about the nature of God and their other peculiar beliefs.

I have carried on numerous conversations with Oneness Pentecostals through the years. In most of these conversations I have posed observations about biblical texts to which no real response is given. Most of these people, however, do not change their beliefs as a result. This is because they have an understanding of the Bible inherited from their ministers and their experience and that becomes the "grid" in which Scripture is placed. If the Bible doesn't fit well, one must simply work harder at making it fit.

My Oneness pastor grew up during the decades in which Oneness theology initially "developed." I recall him once addressing a problematic text in connection with Oneness theology: Revelation 5:6–7. Here the "Lamb" before the throne takes a book out of the "right hand of him who sat on the throne." This scene poses a significant conceptual difficulty for Oneness people. To "see" Jesus, obviously the meaning of the lamb image, walking up to the throne of God and taking a book from God's hand, is very difficult to reconcile with the notion that Jesus is identical with the *one person* of God. My pastor made reference to a discussion on this point with some other ministers many years ago. Since they could not see any apparent solution to this problem, they concluded they would simply have to await further "revelation" from God on how to interpret this text. He claimed that he later "discovered" that the Lamb took the book from the hand of the Church, not the hand of God! This interpretation is so forced and unnatural in the context of Revelation 4–5 that it stretches credulity that one would accept it as compelling. My simple point, however, is that the theology of Oneness was obviously *brought to* Scripture, and anything that did not "fit" well was simply sidelined until someone came up with a good enough explanation.

Oneness Pentecostals, then, live under an *illusion*. The illusion is that the Bible *alone* is the source of their beliefs when, in fact, they accept many things that cannot be demonstrated when limited to the Bible. Additionally, these beliefs are accepted from others who are deemed to have sufficient authority to know whether they are correct or not. To restate, the authority of the Oneness Pentecostal is not the Bible alone, but the Bible *plus* the authority of their pastor and, more generally, the Oneness movement, "confirmed" by personal experience. Of course, this situation is not unique to Oneness Pentecostalism. This illusion is shared by all forms of Christianity that refuse to acknowledge any "source" or mode of authority in addition to Scripture.[†] Catholics, too, accept the authority of their "Tradition," including what the Church says about the Bible, its contents, and its meaning. *The most obvious difference is, however, that Catholics admit this fact.*

Holy Mother Church

Written thousands of years ago, the Bible has been recognized as God's word and transmitted through a long process within a living and active community of people. That community calls itself the *Church.* This Church, down through the centuries, did not make the claim that the Bible *alone* was the grounds of its confidence in God's revelation to the world. Its claim was that the Bible is indeed God's unique revelation, but that it does not stand by itself but is accompanied by the living community of Christ's followers, the Church. This Church is known by its historical identity supplied by its faith and its continuity with earliest Christianity. This continuity is demonstrated by its succession of bishops, originating with

† More precisely, *the* source of all divine revelation is Christ, the eternal "Word." That revelation is transmitted to us in the complementary "modes" of Scripture and Tradition. These two mutually support each other.

the apostles, those chosen by Christ, and expressed in its sacramental life of worship.

The early "bishops" or "overseers" of the Christian churches did not appoint themselves to such offices.[†] They had hands "laid upon" them (1 Tim. 4:14; 2 Tim. 1:6). Since they did not make themselves leaders, their authority was transferred to them from other, recognized authorities. This process began with the apostles who not only laid hands on others to share in their ministry but also established the expectations and requirements for selecting those who would receive this office (e.g., 1 Tim. 3). The function of these bishops was to protect and proclaim the "deposit of faith" inherited from the apostles (1 Tim. 6:20). They were to teach the Faith with authority and rebuke those who taught otherwise (1 Tim. 1:3; 2 Tim. 4:1–4).

Scripture Alone?

In fact, there was *never* a time in the history of early Christianity when the Bible alone functioned as its authority. While the New Testament was still being written, serious doctrinal problems arose and were decisively answered by the living authority of the apostles and those associated with them (e.g., Acts 15:6ff). The New Testament as such did not exist at this time, yet the Church did. The "Bible" of the early Church was the Hebrew scriptures. The apostles did not restrict themselves to its written words, however. The Church would exist a good deal of time without a completed New Testament. It existed, nonetheless.

---

†   I have noticed an interesting phenomenon in this regard in recent years. As some Oneness pastors have aged, they have begun calling themselves "bishops." In the cases with which I am familiar, this title is used to distinguish between themselves and their sons who have become the "pastors" of their congregations.

These remarks are not intended to minimize the importance of Scripture. To the contrary, the Bible is uniquely inspired by God. It is *inseparably* bound to the Church, however, and cannot be correctly appreciated without that historical connection. It was the Church that passed along and protected the sacred texts. It was the Church that recognized the books that were divinely inspired and rejected those lacking this characteristic. It was the Church that watched over the interpretation of Scripture to make sure the Bible's meaning was not hopelessly lost in the morass of interpretations.

If we could travel back in time to the early days of the Christian movement, we would not find a "Bible Only" church. We would find Scripture, to be sure, but Scripture had an authoritative meaning presented by the apostles and their associates, the "elders" and "bishops."

Sometimes Protestant friends object to this claim with Acts 17:11. The Bereans were "more noble" than the Thessalonians because they "examined Scripture daily, to see whether these things were so." It is claimed that even Paul's words were put to the test of Scripture and therefore *only* Scripture should be used as authority in the Church.

One need only read about what Paul preached to the Thessalonians to see why this conclusion does not follow. Paul made claims about Christ's death and resurrection on the basis of the Old Testament (Acts 17:2–3). Unlike the Thessalonians, however, the Bereans actually looked at Scripture to see if Paul's claims were true. Paul made specific claims about what is found in the Old Testament. The Bereans actually looked to see if they were true. If the "Bible Alone" interpretation of this verse is correct, the logical consequence is that Christian authority must be limited to the Old Testament. In truth, the apostles provided an authoritative interpretation of the Hebrew scriptures that was

binding on the Christian community. Some of their interpretations of the Old Testament were later canonized in the
New Testament, and others were transmitted through the
worship and beliefs expressed throughout the Church (both
geographically and historically).

Often 2 Timothy 3:16 is cited in support of the Bible
Alone position. In fact, I have heard public discussions of
this subject in which the full weight of the Bible Alone
case is made to rest on this verse. Paul states that "all
Scripture" is inspired by God and is useful for a variety
of purposes. He further concludes that Scripture makes
the "man of God *perfect*." Since Scripture has the effect of
making one "perfect," we are told, it must be completely
sufficient in every respect. We need nothing else for religious authority.

There are some serious problems with this intepretation.
First, if this text means that Timothy should accept as *absolutely* sufficient the inspired Scripture available to him at
the moment Paul wrote these words, one must reject any
books written after this letter to Timothy. If Paul himself
wrote the letter, a conviction shared by most Pentecostals,
Fundamentalists, and Evangelicals, it must have been written before his death (ca. A.D. 65). It is certainly the case that
a good number of New Testament books had not yet been
written (e.g., John's Gospel, Revelation). If Timothy's Bible
was sufficient to make him entirely perfect and therefore
nothing else was needed, we would have to exclude portions
of the New Testament from our Bible.

Second, the word *perfect* used in this text carries a more
specific meaning than the general notion of Christian "perfection." *Artios*, according to Thayer's Greek lexicon, means
a "special aptitutude for given uses."[32] It is not the word typically used for "perfection" in the New Testament. This fact

is consistent with the context of the verse. Paul's words are written to Timothy, a young bishop and Christian leader. He is called a "man of God," a phrase sometimes obscured in English translations (see 1 Tim. 6:11). A comparison of the uses of the phrase "man of God" throughout the Bible reveals that it is a technical phrase referring to a divinely appointed spokesperson for God. Samuel, for instance, is called a "man of God" (1 Sam. 9:6), as is Moses (Deut. 33:1); an unnamed "man of God" appears to Samson's mother and predicts the birth of her son (Judg. 13:6). We could easily fill pages with similar references. There can be no doubt, once the uses of these words are examined, that the phrase has a precise meaning. It is not a generic reference to Christians or believers in God.

If one appreciates the point of the prior paragraph, the Bible Alone interpretation of 2 Timothy 3:16 immediately fails. Paul is instructing Timothy, a divinely appointed spokesperson for God, to make use of Scripture to teach and rebuke, since they equip him or, to use Thayer's definition, give him a "special aptitutude for given uses." This verse, rather than dispensing with the need for God-given, living spokespersons, affirms that need. Because Scripture is vital in the work of the bishops, for instance, does not make the bishops' office irrelevant or devoid of authority. In this verse, Paul affirms both the authority of the bishops and the authority of Scripture.

Given that the two texts discussed above are the primary ones used to support the Bible Alone position, it is hard to avoid the ironic conclusion that the Bible itself does not support the Bible Alone position. Again, we fully agree that the Bible is inspired, given by God, and authoritative. What we deny is that it stands alone as the Church's authority. It must be accompanied by "men of God," to use biblical language.

The rise of Protestantism brought with it the naïve belief that Scripture alone could function as the sole authority for Christian faith. The Reformers and their successors painfully realized, in time, that this belief is unworkable. While they did break away from the Catholic Church, they unconsciously brought with them an entire framework for understanding what Scripture is and what it means. That framework was crucial; without it, other frameworks would be supplied and result in a host of redefinitions of Christianity. The seemingly endless mass of such reinterpretations litter the history of modern Christianity.

The great Reformers, particularly Luther and Calvin, *never* consistently practiced the theory that Scripture alone is the source of Christian faith. They always, at least implicitly, accepted the traditional reading of Scripture with the exception of those topics they chose to dispute. Alister McGrath, a noted contemporary Evangelical theologian and Reformation historian, notes this fact while speaking of the magisterial Reformers in contrast to the "radicals":

> But none, it must be emphasized, was prepared to abandon the concept of a traditional interpretation of Scripture in favor of the radical alternative. As Luther gloomily observed, *the inevitable result of such an approach was chaos, a "new Babel."*[33]

The Need for Context

The Bible, in order to function as a true authority, must come to us within a framework that allows us to (a) recognize its origin, extent, and authority and (b) properly read its contents. The Catholic faith, from the very beginning, has professed both the authority of Scripture and a divinely given context or framework in which to properly read and understand its message. We may observe this in the

New Testament itself during those occasions the apostles settled disputes about the meaning of Christianity with a definitive judgment. In a certain sense, the New Testament books themselves, at least many of them, are an exercise of apostolic authority in providing an authoritative explanation and interpretation of Christian faith. We continue to observe this same approach to authority in the years and decades following the writing of the biblical books. The text that, many years ago, captured my attention in this regard is found in the writings of the great second-century apologist, Irenaeus:

> It is within the power of all, therefore, in every church, who may wish to see the truth, to contemplate clearly the Tradition of the apostles manifested throughout the whole world; and *we are in a position to reckon up those who were by the apostles instituted bishops in the churches, and [to demonstrate] the succession of these men to our own times*; those who neither taught nor knew of anything like what these [heretics] rave about . . . Since, however, it would be very tedious, in such a volume as this, to reckon up the successions of all the churches . . . we do this, I say, by indicating that Tradition derived from the apostles, of the very great, the very ancient, and universally known Church founded and organized at Rome by the two most glorious apostles, Peter and Paul; as also [by pointing out] the faith preached to men, *which comes down to our time by means of the succession of the bishops.* For it is a matter of necessity that every church should agree with this Church, on account of its preeminent authority, that is, the faithful everywhere, inasmuch as the apostolical tradition has been preserved continuously by those [faithful men] who exist everywhere.[34]

This text, although strikingly "Catholic," is by no means unique. It is easy to find the same ideas scattered throughout early Christian literature; so much so, we must conclude that the notion of apostolic succession is an integral part of early Christianity. J.N.D. Kelly, noted patristics scholar, summarizes the evidence from the Nicene era regarding the Church's understanding of the relationship between Scripture and Tradition:

> The ancient idea that the Church alone, in virtue of being the home of the Spirit and having preserved the authentic apostolic testimony in her rule of faith, liturgical action, and general witness, *possesses the indispensable key to Scripture*, continued to operate as powerful as in the days of Irenaeus and Tertullian . . . Hilary insisted that only those who accept the Church's teaching can comprehend what the Bible is getting at . . . Throughout the whole period Scripture and Tradition ranked as complementary authorities . . . If Scripture was abundantly sufficient in principle, *Tradition was recognized as the surest clue to its interpretation.*[35]

The early Christian Church did not maintain its unique identity and faith by appeal to Scripture alone. They appealed to both Scripture and the apostolic Tradition passed along in unbroken succession through the bishops. This succession of bishops provided a living context in which the Bible's true meaning was preserved, lived, developed, and recognized. We affectionately speak of the *source* of these actions as our "Mother." Mary, the mother of our Lord, "pondered" the mysteries of Christ within her heart, and a savior was born into the darkness of this world. So, too, the *Church*, complete with its ministry guided by the Spirit and protected by

God, "ponders" the mysteries of faith and continually brings
Christ into the world in *her* proclamation and celebration of
those mysteries. Christ promised that the Spirit would guide
the apostles into "all the truth" (John 16:13). In spite of human frailty and fallibility, Christ's promise to the apostles
echoes through the centuries in the Church that flows with
unbroken succession from the apostles.

Often Catholics are ridiculed for their belief in the infal-
libility of the Church. Our critics often forget that they, too,
believe that God caused, by inspiration, the biblical writers
to produce infallible documents, according to their doctrine
of inerrancy. In principle, then, we both acknowledge God
can and *has* caused fallible men to write (or speak) infallibly.

Our Protestant friends, including Oneness Pentecostals,
assert the Bible is their final and sole authority in all matters.
Catholics, on the other hand, accept the authority of Scripture in union with the Church that assures us, by unbroken
succession from the apostles, of what the Bible is, what it
means, and how it should be lived. The distinct advantage
of the Catholic position is multifaceted.

First, it has the advantage of mirroring the Church of
the first century. With its living authority inherited from
the apostles, the Catholic Church is truly *apostolic*. Second,
it has the advantage of acknowledging its debt to the historical Church. Protestants, in varying degrees, must distance
themselves from the authority of the historical Church and
are thereby left without good answers to the various questions
already posed in this chapter. Third, the Catholic position
makes sense out of real, everyday human life. Not everyone
is a Bible scholar or historian. Catholics believe the word of
the Church, our mother. Protestants believe the words of the
Bible but fail to give credit to the Church for protecting it,
recognizing it, and passing along its meaning. Fourth, this

position allows us to maintain the highest regard for Scripture as the word of God. God so desired to communicate himself to the world that he not only gave us the Bible, but assured us of its proper extent and meaning by linking it to a community of faith with a living authority that complements the unique authority of the Bible.

Peter and the Church's Survival

Jesus promised that the Church would never die: "Upon this rock I will build my Church; *and the gates of Hades shall not overpower it*" (Matt. 16:18). *Hades*, a Greek word for the abode of the dead, signifies death. Jesus promised that death would not overcome the Church. It *will* survive, and its survival is tied directly to the promises made to Peter.

Doubtless it is true that many "churches" have come and gone through the centuries. Others have lost their original meaning. Others have died only to later arise in some other form. The survival of Christ's Church is linked to the "keys of the kingdom" entrusted to Peter. The emphasis on Peter in this text and others points to an inevitable conclusion: Jesus singled Peter out and gave him a unique role in strengthening and guiding the ancient Church established by him (Luke 22:31-32, John 21:15-17). That much, to my mind, is indisputable. Those who reject the unique place given to Peter in the Gospels, and also reflected in the book of Acts, typically do so for purely polemical reasons.

What is not often seen, however, is that Peter's role in the Church *must* continue throughout the centuries. This is implied in Matthew 16:17–19 in two important ways. First, the promises made to Peter are tied to the Church's endurance and its victory over death. If the Church will never die on account of the authority entrusted to Peter, it follows that Peter's authority will endure to the end of time.

There is a great problem, however: Peter died! The solution to this problem is found in a second observation: the *keys* of the kingdom. *Keys* are an ancient symbol of authority, just as they carry similar meaning today. If I possess the keys to something, I have some measure of authority over it (e.g., Rev. 1:18, 3:7). They also carry the connotation of an authority that is transferable to another (Isa. 22:15ff).[36]

In light of the fact that Peter died, we must ask, who inherited the "keys" entrusted to him by Christ? We already know the answer from Irenaeus and others. The successors of Peter, the bishops of Rome, the city in which Peter died, inherited that unique authority. We affectionately call Peter's successor the *pope*, or *papa*.

On two occasions I have walked beneath the Basilica of St. Peter on the pre-Christian road through a cemetery on the Vatican hill. That road, surrounded by ancient tombs and masoleums, leads to the tomb directly beneath the basilica's main altar. Strong evidence supports the conclusion that this tomb is that of the apostle Peter. There is little doubt that Peter died under the persecution of Emperor Nero around the year A.D. 65. There is also abundant reason to believe that the unique role of Peter, the "rock" chosen by Christ, lived on in the bishops of the Church of Rome. The ancient Christians certainly believed this to be the case.

Although the Catholic Church is typically vilified by Oneness Pentecostals, I discovered that the most precious truths I believed as a youth were not only shared in common with Catholicism but were more fully embraced there. I discovered that my love of the Bible is more solidly grounded within Catholicism, since I have a more complete understanding and explanation of *why* we accept the Bible as we do. My interpretation of the Bible is no longer an *individualistic* one based on someone who lived in 1901 or some other recent moment in history. I fully acknowledge that I read the Bible within a received context and framework for understanding. The reality is that *everyone* does this. The question one must answer is, "Why choose one framework over another?" The Catholic answer is 2,000 years old. It is reflected in every Christian century. Unlike Oneness Pentecostalism, Catholicism has no need to speak of the lost "truth" of Christianity.

In light of the fact that I believe Jesus is Messiah and Son of God and that he provided fully for our salvation, I have no choice but to embrace the Church as my "mother." The same may be said of my love of Scripture. I would not know what Scripture is without the Church, a point Augustine loved to emphasize. Even though, as a youth, I was ignorant of the inseparable relationship that exists between the Bible and the Church, it was still true. Those who would cling to the Bible without clinging to the Church are, in light of the historical facts, inconsistent.

One might wish his parents were something other than what they are, but the fact remains, they are his parents. The "wish" that things were different does not change the debt owed to them for one's very life. Similarly, one may find the Catholic Church "unattractive," for whatever reason. The fact is, though, that all Christians owe a debt to her that is rarely appreciated and acknowledged. Greater familiarity and openness to the Church, however, often dispels misconceptions and fosters a growing love of the beauties of the Catholic faith.

Beware of Distortions

I never met a Oneness Pentecostal who had even a basic grasp of Catholic beliefs. This was, I'm sure, because they typically do not feel Catholicism is worthy of study. It is also because they feel that Catholicism is so obviously flawed on so many matters that it would be foolish to waste time studying it.

This was my conviction, too, for much of my youth and some of my young adult life. I found, however, that there were good reasons for everything the Catholic Church formally professes. I discovered biblical texts that certainly *can* be read from a Catholic perspective. The grave "evils" of confession (John 20:23), purgatory (1 Cor. 3:11–15), "prayers" to saints (Heb. 12:23–24), emphasis on Mary (Luke 1:42ff), the papacy (Matt. 16:17ff), and a host of other issues, were never accurately presented and their biblical basis neglected.

I recall a conversation with a middle-aged lady standing in an aisle of an Evangelical bookstore. I had known this lady for some time. She was particularly hostile to Catholic beliefs. In fact, on that occasion she was purchasing a large number of anti-Catholic tracts that she planned to distribute to as many Catholics as she could find. She was raised in a nominal Catholic family, fell away from her upbringing, and later discovered Pentecostalism. Her newfound enthusiasm for this brand of Christian faith expressed itself in a rather angry assualt on Catholicism. She had learned of my "leanings" toward Catholicism and sought to expose the great evils of the Church.

"The Bible says nothing about purgatory!" she insisted. I directed her to 1 Corinthians 3:11–15. Here, I explained, St. Paul writes of a coming "Day" of Judgment when our works will be tested "by fire." Some will "suffer loss," by means of "fire," but will, nonetheless, be "saved." Since these persons are "saved," this text cannot be describing hell. It seems reasonable, I insisted, that our lives will undergo a judgment that will purify us of all "works" that are not of enduring value. This purifying Judgment makes us internally "fit" for the joys of heaven. This is little different, it seems to me, from the Catholic teaching regarding purgatory.

She struggled to offer a reply. Paul's teachings simply did not fit her theology. She understood salvation as a moment in time in which God forgives us and makes us a "new creation." The Final Judgment pertains to whether or not I have had that experience, not the works I have done. Paul's letter does not fit this understanding of what happens when our present life is over. After pressing her for some time, she finally surprised me by replying, "Well, that's Paul's writings. Jesus never taught that." I think she realized how ridiculous this reply was while she uttered it. It was remarkable, though, to see a committed Evangelical resort to questioning the authority of Scripture itself all in an effort to avoid a Catholic reading of the Bible!

On another occasion, a friend of mine, also raised in the Oneness movement, questioned me about the rosary. He saw it, predictably, as a horrible and idolatrous form of prayer. After all, we pray the "Hail Mary" ten times more than any prayer addressed directly to God or Christ! I gave him a pamphlet on the rosary and explained that the Hail Mary provides the "background" to a series of meditations on the various "mysteries" of the life, death, resurrection, and ascension of Christ. Mary is invoked simply as a "helper" in this reflection on her son. Our prayer is an attempt to view Christ through the humble and open disposition of Mary. I explained to my friend that my experience of the rosary, rather than distracting me from Christ, enhanced my devotion to him. After our conversation, he was willing to try it for himself. He later admitted that this form of prayer was richly rewarding.

Many pages could be filled with similar stories. I am convinced that, with very few exceptions, people do not hate Catholicism because they truly understand its teachings but, rather, because they have simply misunderstood them.

Again, I found the Bible *can* honestly be interpreted in support of Catholic beliefs. I know of *nothing* the Church formally teaches that cannot be grounded in the Bible. While still in the world of Protestant Christianity, my awareness of this fact resulted in a fundamental choice. My choice was either to maintain *my* interpretation of the Bible by rejecting the Catholic context, a choice that carries grave consequences on other matters discussed in this chapter, or I could choose to immerse myself within the Catholic context. Many times, those so-called "grave evils" that Protestants find within Catholicism actually become beautiful when truly understood. Although it is beyond our task in this work to address the many questions that might be posed, one can do no better than read the Church's faith in her own words in the *Catechism of the Catholic Church*. This beautiful and accurate summary of Catholic faith is sufficient to dispel countless misunderstandings and unveil the real meaning of Catholic faith.[†]

Conclusion

I am grateful for my years within Pentecostalism. I learned much from my teachers and friends. I do not doubt for one moment the deep sincerity of Oneness believers. Indeed, there are many things we share in common. We certainly appreciate their firm belief in one God and the full divinity of Jesus Christ, despite important differences in our full explanations of these beliefs. We admire their love of the Bible and their fervent preaching of its contents. We admire their firm commitment to dedicate their whole lives to God; without doubt, they express their commitment in many admirable ways.

As we have seen, however, there are many weaknesses. All these weaknesses have a common root: *disregard of apostolic*

[†] There are many other invaluable works available. The list is much too long to include here. I would mention Karl Keating's book *Catholicism and Fundamentalism* (San Francisco: Ignatius Press, 1988) as a wonderful response to the many Fundamentalist works against Catholicism, including fine chapters answering many of the typical objections posed against our faith. This book was especially valuable in my own journey, in its early chapters that analyze and respond to popular anti-Catholic spokespersons and literature, much of which influenced me as a young man.

authority. It is ironic that a movement that prides itself on its apostolicity would fail to see that the apostolic Church followed the authority of Christ's chosen apostles. Those apostles passed along their oversight to successors who, together with the successor of Peter, protected the Faith through the centuries. Oneness Pentecostalism, in some ways, is unique but it is, at root, the reemergence of a heresy that was evaluated and rejected long ago because of its deficiencies when placed in contrast to the apostolic Faith. The real issue is not whether a skilled Oneness debater can "answer" challenges to his understanding of the Bible, or whether a Catholic debater can do the same. I have lived long enough to know that, if one is skilled and determined enough, anything can be argued. One must, in the depths of his heart, answer whether or not it is reasonable to believe God chose this as our path to understand Christian faith. I find the Catholic answer supremely reasonable but that of Protestantism seriously deficient.

Decades ago, I stood with two other Evangelical Christian "apologists" on the steps of the famous tower at the University of Texas (Austin). We were answering questions about our faith from several hundred students who had gathered to listen to the lively exchange of ideas. One young lady stood up to the microphone and pointed her finger at me. She asked, "I want *you* to answer a question for me. We listen to many people tell us their version of what is true. I want to know, *why should I accept your interpretation of the Bible?*" I don't recall what I told her. What I do recall is the three-hour drive to Houston that night. Her question haunted me. Why should anyone listen to *me*? A profound sense of how small and insignificant I am swept over me. *Why should anyone listen to me?*

The *only* good reason anyone should listen to me, I have come to believe, is because what I say is part of a 2,000-year chorus to which I have joined my voice. No one should believe anything because *I* say it. There is good reason to believe it because *we* say it, however. I stand with the Church that has endured, against all odds, the test of time. At the fount of the Church's faith stand Christ and his chosen apostles and a promise that the Church will never die. There are solid reasons to accept these claims.

For those who want to know why they should follow Christ, I answer with Jesus' words, "Come and see" (John 1:39). The more I "stay with" Jesus, the more I am led to agree with Philip: "We have found him of whom Moses in the law, and also the prophets, wrote" (John 1:45). It is not possible, however, to be with Christ and yet reject his Church. Saul of Tarsus, on his way to persecute the Christians of Damascus, was confronted by Christ who declared, "Saul, why do you persecute *me*?" Since the Church is mystically united with Christ, we cannot sever their bond. To persecute the Church is to persecute Christ.

In conclusion, the Oneness interpretation of the Bible will, in time, pass away. I suppose it will reemerge in various forms throughout coming ages, presuming our Lord does not bring a more prompt end to our pilgrim journey. I am fully confident, however, that the faith in the Triune God and, more generally, the faith professed by the Catholic Church, will endure until that faith is immersed into the blessedness of the unending life of love for which we were made. Then we shall "*know* as also we are known" (1 Cor. 13:12; 1 John 3:2).

About the Author

Mark McNeil is the assistant principal for formation and a member of the theology department at Strake Jesuit College Preparatory, where he has taught since 2000. He has earned master's degrees in Scripture, theology, and philosophy. Mark also teaches theology part-time at the University of St. Thomas and has spoken at parishes and conferences across the Houston area and throughout the country. Mark was received into the Catholic Church in 1999. Mark and his wife, Patti, along with their children, are active parishioners at St. Luke the Evangelist parish in Houston, Texas.

Endnotes

1   Fred Foster, *Their Story: Twentieth Century Pentecostals* (Hazelwood, MO: Word Aflame Press, 1965), 88-90.

2   See Jean-Pierre Torrell, O.P., *Saint Thomas Aquinas: Spiritual Master*, v. 2 (Washington, DC: Catholic University of America Press, 2003), 49-52.

3   See J.B. Lightfoot and J.R. Harmer, eds., *The Apostolic Fathers* (Berkeley: Apocryfile Press, 2004), 259.

4   Bernard, *The New Birth*, 266.

5   David K. Bernard, *The Oneness of God* (Weldon Spring, MO: Pentecostal Publishing House, 1986), 92.

6   See Ratzinger, *Jesus of Nazareth*.

7   Bernard, *The Oneness of God*, 144.

8   Bernard, 142-3.

9   Bernard, *The Oneness of God*, 183-4, emphasis added.

10 Ibid.

11 See D.A. Carson, *The Gospel According to John* (Grand Rapids, MI: Eerdmans, 1991), 117.

12 Bernard, *The Oneness of God*, 60-61.

13 Bernard, *The Oneness of God*, 17.

14 Nicolas of Cusa (1401-1464). See discussion of this point in Armand Maurer, *Medieval Philosophy* (Toronto: Pontifical Institute of Mediaeval Studies, 1982), 310ff.

15 Gordon Magee, *Is Jesus in the Godhead or Is the Godhead in Jesus?* (Hazelwood, MO: Word Aflame, 1989), 18.

16 Magee, *Is Jesus in the Godhead,* 18.

17 Bernard, *The Oneness of God*, 171.

18 Bernard, *The Oneness of God*, 90.

19 C.F. Keil and F. Delitzsch, *Commentary on the Old Testament* (Grand Rapids, MI: Eerdmans: 1982 reprint), 10:253.

20 Bernard, *The Oneness of God*, 127.

21 Bernard, *The Oneness of God*, 104.

22 Bernard, *The Oneness of God*, 105.

23 Bernard, *The Oneness of God*, 27.

24 Yves Congar, *I Believe in the Holy Spirit*, vol. 1 (New York: Crossroad, 1983), vii.

25 Bernard, *The Oneness of God*, 128.

26 Ibid.

27 Bernard, *The Oneness of God*, 195-196.

28 Bernard, *The Oneness of God*, 196.

29 *Catechism of the Catholic Church* (1994), 234.

30 Bernard, *The New Birth*, 218.

31 Stanley M. Burgess, "Evidence of the Spirit: The Medieval and Modern Western Churches," in Gary B. McBee, ed., *Initial Evidence: Historical and Biblical Perspectives on the Pentecostal Doctrine of Spirit Baptism* (Eugene: Wipf and Stock, 2008), 37 (emphasis added).

32 Joseph Henry Thayer, *The Greek-English Lexicon of the New Testament*, 4th ed. (London: T & T Clark, 1901), 75. See also Bauer, Arndt, and Gingrich, *A Greek-English Lexicon*

of the New Testament and Other Early Christian Literature, 2nd ed. (Chicago: Univ. of Chicago Press, 1979), 110.

33 Alister E. McGrath, *Reformation Thought: An Introduction* (Ada, MI: Baker, 1988), 146.

34 Irenaeus, *Against Heresies*, III.3. Roberts and Donaldson, eds., *Ante-Nicene Fathers*, vol. 1 (Grand Rapids, MI: Eerdmans, 1987 reprint).

35 J.N.D. Kelly, *Early Christian Doctrines, Rev. ed.* (New York: Harper Collins, 1978), 47-8 (emphasis added).

36 W.F. Albright and C.S. Mann, *The Anchor Bible: Matthew* (New York: Doubleday, 1971), 196.